FINDING THEIR STRIDE

Sally Pont

FINDING THEIR STRIDE

A Team of Young Runners Races to the Finish

HARCOURT BRACE & COMPANY

New York   San Diego   London

Library of Congress Cataloging-in-Publication Data
Pont, Sally.
Finding their stride: a team of young runners races
to the finish/by Sally Pont.—1st ed.
p.   cm.
ISBN 0-15-100347-5
1. Moravian Academy (Bethlehem, Pa.)—Track-athletics.
2. Runners—Pennsylvania—Biography.   3. Pont, Sally.   I. Title.
GV1060.62.P4P65   1999
796.42′0922—dc21   98-50205

Designed by BTD   Text set in Simoncini Garamond
Printed in the United States of America
First edition   E   D   C   B   A

To my father, Richard Pont,
the real coach

Acknowledgments

Shy, girlish gratitude to my mentor, Paul West.

Awestruck thanks to my editor, Jane Isay, who, with white steel and feathers, poked and tickled me through this project.

Hugs all 'round to the members of the Moravian Academy community whose support instilled in me the desire to celebrate the place: the Kozinn family, Joe Chandler, Greg Byala, Marilyn Albarelli, Kate Steciw, Max Smith, and Fred Vasta.

Apologies and promises of future writing to those who deserved much more than a mere mention in this work, especially Mike Mescher, smack-talking romantic; Kate Webbink, quiet lover of nature; Holly Macko, fierce friend; and Bryan Hollingsworth, true companion.

Props to runners past and present who, as a result of the runner's nemesis—time and space—will not find their own sinuous stories in this book: Matt Young, Tanya Clark, Winston Eaton, Hilary Berseth, Christine Whitney, and Chris Balshi.

Finally and especially, to my ever-patient husband Steve, so much love.

FINDING THEIR STRIDE

Gretchen and Leyla arrive first, lugging Tupperware. They are slim and fragile as origami. Their skin, fresh from showers, is smooth and brown. A window over the kitchen table, facing west, breathes light on the crests of their hair. They are eager to please, clamoring in birdlike voices to help. I set them to chopping vegetables. After they pile their containers on the table, the transparent sides revealing neatly stacked cookies and brownies, paper towels between layers, they make quick work of some pulpy tomatoes and a few yellow peppers. Then they look at me with large eyes, pleading to do more. I turn my back on them not because I want to, but to pull, from the cabinet by the stove, pots and lids that tumble and thump on the floor.

Heels in the stairwell clip-clip to the door of my apartment. A club of chipper freshmen, Sara, Holly, and Rachel, bursts in, midconversation—Sara and Rachel artsy and tough in Doc Martens, Holly softer, sweeter, with dimples. They are all noticeably narrow, as runners should be, even in their loose skater clothes. Holly, though, is the strongest of the three and should, quite easily, be among the top five on their cross country team. Because I have water running into two of the pots to boil for spaghetti, I can't really hear their greeting, and they can't really hear my reply. They have food and drink that they toss on the table, then they chatter away, wandering into the living room to poke through the CD collection and wait for the rest of their team to arrive.

They are here to eat because the pleasure of food now might dull the pain of racing five kilometers tomorrow. Pain is clever, though. From the first stride, it spelunks through the body, mining deep. It begins in the cavern of the head with a hammered ringing, shimmies down the larynx, scuffs the stomach, swings from hamstrings, digs its spiked heels into ankles, then catapults back up to the melting knees, the roasting heart, and the head again, where the ringing has become the howl of the dog.

In one minute, pain completes this circuit, taking bites as it goes. For Leyla and Gretchen, that carousel of pain will go around twenty-four times during tomorrow's race. So now they are in my kitchen, buttering bread.

Soundlessly, Dave appears with a white laundry basket of produce from his family's farm. It is full of a tough, leafy vegetable, some tubers with dry dirt clinging, and several dozen cherry tomatoes. A few have split, and carmine juice swirls at the bottom of the basket.

"That's broccoli rabe, isn't it?" I ask, indicating the thick, spiky leaves.

"No, but I don't know what it is." His feathery hair sifting from side to side, he nods as if he is gaining points for caution. In his thrift-store pants and ocher shirt, he looks like a young Kerouac.

"Look, look." I point to a burst of pale green spores with the wooden spoon I am clutching. "There's the broccoli."

"No," he insists. He knows that we are arguing not about vegetables, but about language. I wonder if I think Dave is a great runner simply because I admire his intellect. At a stalemate, we face each other, I with my stained spoon, Dave with his silence. In my mind, I acknowledge he is right.

While Dave vanishes into the whirl of the living

room, I instruct Gretchen to chop some of his veggies for the salad. She plucks feathery stems from the basket, tomatoes dangling like tiny bells.

The water on the stove rumbles but is not quite boiling. I turn the heat down a bit and swirl golden oil into the dancing water, not knowing when the whole team will assemble, ready to eat their prerace pasta. The oven rocks and guffaws. Eyeing the water, I wrap aluminum foil around loaves of buttered bread. As I am searching for my pot holders, a voice calls hello behind me—Sam George.

"Ms. Pont," he starts in with the practical: "When do we eat? When do we eat?" He is the captain; he eats, and does everything else, passionately. With long fingers, he rests a pie on the counter in front of me. Flustered, I stutter, "Soon, it'll be ready soon. Soon." Sam, over a foot taller than me, pats my head. Because his charm is undiluted, he gets away with it.

Nervous footsteps dash in and around the building, thumping up the wrong corridor, turning around, then slinking back again, listening at the door.

"Sam, someone's lost," I say. "Go see who that is."

I stir the sauce. Thick bubbles balloon the surface then sink under their own weight. One bursts and sends tomato splattering across the stove top. The red droplets sizzle and brown along the edges. Flecks of oregano blacken and stick.

The door opens and slams, opens and slams. More voices puncture the smells of the kitchen. "I have knives and forks," says Rajeev; "I have Coke," says Nimish. "Where can we put them?" they ask in unison, as if they have rehearsed. Rajeev is more handsome, Nimish more humorous, but the two have, by choice, been linked like a pair of cymbals. Even in races, they run together, thin legs pedaling away. As they run, they chronicle for each other, in whispers, the exact location of their pain. That way, they know how far they have gone and how far they have left to run.

"Put them wherever you can," I reply. The counters are strewn with objects useful and useless, but there's no time to tidy. On the cluttered table, they somehow find room. The kitchen is full of bodies, casting Giacometti shadows, the living room is full of pitched voices, bickering and flirting. No one seems at all worried about tomorrow's race.

I focus on the necessity of food and empty four boxes of spaghetti. It bends and swirls in the dark, frothy water.

Though I believe in this sacrament of sharing supper, I know that, once again, I have taken on too much. Neither my kitchen nor my mind is equipped to feed thirty. The stove, all burners going now, red coils slightly akimbo, holds me transfixed out of electric panic. If I leave it, disaster will surely strike—burning, spilling, sweeping damage, the loss of human lives—on a level worthy of the evening news. My eyes dart maniacally from pot to pot, my hands stirring here, adjusting heat there, my mind all the while conscious of the conversations behind me. I imagine mothers come undone at this containment because they want to control their children. I simply want to join mine, to converse, to laugh, and then to be fed. Nevertheless, I keep my chest to the stove, arms up, ready for earthquakes, tornadoes, overcooked noodles and bland sauce.

Exclamations greet Kate Webbink's platter of cannoli. She smiles shyly, covering her braces. With their cellophane wrapping, the sweets are bright as flowers in a bouquet. I smile at the pattern: this year, more girls on the team, therefore more desserts at the spaghetti dinner that signals the birth of the season.

With long-distance runners, especially young ones, the desire to eat is incessant. They devour hundreds of grams of fat and several thousand calories, regardless of recommended daily allowances. Though Leyla and Gretchen, converts to cross country from tennis and field hockey, are low-fat eaters (the nineties' version of the calorie counter), knowledgeable about the fat content of snacks, meats, even fruits, they get dreamy when the subject of ice cream comes up. But whenever they profess their passion for fresh fruits and their discomfort with McDonald's, all the boys and the rest of the girls are incredulous.

Eyes glaring over their glasses, Nimish and Rajeev move in on me with plates up, shifting slightly from side to side, backward and forward. Though I am small, they are smaller: under ninety pounds; I swat them away. The door again clicks open and closed. Paper bags rustle. Coke fizzles in plastic cups.

"Can I heat up the garlic bread?" someone asks.

Someone hands me a bag of pretossed Caesar salad.

"I have a cheesecake!"

Body parts dance all around me.

"Ms. Pont!" Sam's voice erupts from the living room. "Can we listen to music?"

Good, I think. They can distract themselves till the pasta is done. "Sure, Sam!"

When the music kicks in, loud enough for a rave, it is Ani DiFranco snarling: "Fuck you, and your untouchable face. Fuck you, for existing in the first place." I wince. Sam's DJing skills are impeccable.

Face pink from the furiously boiling water, I throw a string of spaghetti against the wall. It sticks. With my hands sausaged into mitts, I lift a pot and take it to the sink where a colander awaits. I empty the spaghetti into it. When the water rises and subsides, I drizzle oil into the noodles and toss them up.

One of my frequent fibs is that I'm a great cook. I'm no such thing. Sometimes I'm a lucky cook, turning things out that are tasty and lovely simply because food can be that way. Most of the time, I'm nervous about preparing food because I am afraid of failure. With my cross country team, though, my fear is more complex. I love them so much—too much, I know—that I want to feed them ambrosia, manna, fishes and loaves . . . mythic foods.

Arms disjointed from bodies hold up flimsy plastic plates. With two spoons, I pull slippery noodles from the colander then drop them, pell-mell, onto the plates. Fingers catch loose skeins, and the arms move away to ladle their own sauce.

Something is burning. Sam has placed his plate on a hot burner, and it vaporizes while spaghetti liquefies and conforms to the coils. As I quickly scrape with a knife, scooping hot, pasty gunk into a paper towel, Sam holds the plate up to his face as a postmodern mask.

"I'm keeping this!" he says, then secures a fresh plate. He serves himself, piling pasta higher than before.

I am now alone in the kitchen. I cut a piece of bread from the loaf I baked the night before and butter it. Outside the window, the geese gather on Green Pond, their muscular wings turbulent, hailing early fall with hungry shrieks. I pour another full pot into the colander and serve the second round; Nimish and Rajeev come back for thirds.

It is the week before school begins as well as the day before the first race, one of those hectic times in which everyone is busy but unproductive. Sam Cohen, then, is the last to arrive, worn out from his duties as senior class president, which today meant helping run orientation for new students. His crisp shirt is neatly tucked into trousers, his hair, freshly cut, bristles cheerfully—but he seems otherwise burdened: from his responsibility, from his recent service project in Virgin Gorda, where he built houses for the homeless, and from thoughts of the future. He says he isn't hungry. His shoulders fold like the wings of a tired bird. He paces the kitchen before entering the fracas in the living room. I sense that he, like most of the team, is beginning the season with one thought dominant in his mind: when will it end?

The next day's race, against teams both literally and figuratively out of our league—East Stroudsburg, Stroudsburg, Pocono Mountain, and four others—will not be easy. Their schools, located in surrounding and distant towns, are four or five times the size of Moravian Academy. With a larger student pool to draw from, their teams are bulky and taut with talent. Except for this race, at the beginning of the season, and the District XI race, at the conclusion, they compete primarily against each other, rather than us, in either the Colonial or Mountain Valley Leagues, while we most often face other small independent schools in the Penn-Jersey League.

Tonight, pasta in their bellies, Gretchen and Leyla might feel that they can win against such competition, but tomorrow? Will they be afraid?

Fear is sensing that the world is not the way we want it to be, we are not the people we want to be. We conjure myths about ourselves—we are the superheroes of Strength or Beauty or Cool—and believe in them soundly until the instant they are critiqued. Then we begin to tremble. The fear that comes before a race, specifically, is the desire to win coupled with the sense that, most likely, victory is out of the question. Although no fear is easy to express, runners are hesitant to articulate the terror that precedes a race. Reactions to such a confession are always so trivial, so insulting. At their most distilled, those responses become the following question: *Then why do you run?*

Bryan, pouring more soda, has just asked just that of Katie Hartman, who has run for three years. He is new to the team, but swift, with a muscular gait and curly hair bobbing as he runs. She shrugs her angular shoulders. When she was a freshman, the girls' team—the few times the five runners required to qualify as a full team actually assembled—consistently lost. Her pale, freckled face frowns. "I don't know. I hate to run."

"So do I," says Bryan. He sips contemplatively from his Coke. He and Katie, sensing I hear, glance over at me nervously.

"I hate it, too," I say.

They don't appear to be surprised. In just two weeks of practice, Bryan has found himself eye to eye with the strange horror of running. Katie, too; though the girls' team has tripled in size, fear still steps, cold as a ghost, into the ranks.

The loathing has little to do with physical pain. Pain is, like time, a backdrop to running. The hatred, rather, is spurred, almost completely, by the fear prior to a race. That fear corrodes character. It threatens to prevent the first step.

Sam Cohen is neither more nor less afraid about tomorrow's race than anyone else. That he missed the two weeks of preseason adds to his anxiety, but those two weeks, for many, constructed anxiety, nerve ending by nerve ending. The boys are burdened by the legacy of past teams, particularly last year's, with two runners placing so high in the District XI race that they qualified for the state championship; the girls gulp in the airless absence of a legacy, wishing for the burden. Josh is nursing acute pains in his foot that will not go away; Gretchen is brushing against the anguish of competition; some wonder whether they can finish a five-kilometer race at all.

A WEEK AGO, nerves itched and tingled due to the five-K race at the Blue Valley Farm Show, a sunset "fun run" beginning and ending near tents ripe with sheep and Black Angus cattle. Against folks from the community, young and old, most of our team was running, including me.

Nerves whimpered quietly. Gretchen's family was there. Dave wasn't ready. Tom was. Moreover, numbers safety-pinned to chests meant business. Almost all of them, though, chatted and laughed beforehand. Of Josh, however, fear took possession. Though he had never run competitively before, he had emerged during preseason as a natural—light and quick, with excellent form and an eagerness to please. He did push-ups elegantly, soundlessly. Before the road race, he talked to me a great deal, asking me what he should do. I told him to stick with me.

The day seemed shady and pleasant when several of us met in the parking lot in front of Snyder House at Moravian Academy. In Pen Argyl, though, the site of the farm show, the August sun was potent, heating the roofs of parked cars, the dust of the parking lot, the thick hides of the prize-winning steers. After paying our ten-dollar registration fee and picking up our T-shirts, we scattered, wedging ourselves into the slivers of violet shade cast by signs and tents. Finally, I gathered the team and we went for a warm-up run around the first leg of the course.

I, too, joined the worriers when Sam George was late, but he arrived as we were stretching. Sam, in black shorts, blacker tank top, worn black socks, and a red bandanna, was intimidating. Because he had done a lot of yoga over the summer, his body was strong. In the past, he was a vocal breather. This season, from the start, he scarcely opened his mouth. Sam, unlike the rest of us, felt no fear. He was faithful to his personal mythology.

For the first mile, a gradual uphill into a residential neighborhood, Josh ran at my elbow, exhaling his fear. It emitted a smell like limes, thin but forceful. "Relax your arms," I told him. "Concentrate on your breathing." He couldn't hear me. He was too focused on calculating how many steps remained. His footfalls were irregular, and his breathing grew harsher and harsher.

At the one-mile mark, I had to leave him. Though I hated to do it, I wondered if my presence only offered added pressure. "I'm gonna pick up my pace," I panted out. He waved halfheartedly.

For four or five minutes, I crept up to Sam George's long shadow and stayed there, drawing strength from him. The third mile was downhill, shaded. I let my arms carry me to the finish line.

Not far behind me, Josh kicked it in, breathing rhythmically. His brow, however, was still furrowed in fear. One hand pressed into his ribs to check his breathing, he walked, duckfooted, away from the finish line. He came close to me, leaning his shoulder toward mine.

"Ms. Pont, my foot really hurts."

"It's a tough course," I responded, placing thumb and forefinger into the grooves of his collarbone. "All that pavement. Your feet are gonna really pound on that downhill at the end."

Lifting his jawline so his eyes met mine, he nodded sharply, then walked light-footed to get a cup of water. When he did so, he transferred his fear to me. I was terrified at the thought of losing Josh to injury, and the fear crept over me the way water spreads across a surface, invisible except at certain angles. I glanced nervously at Josh, who was standing at a table where a man poured water, willy-nilly, into Dixie cups. Josh watched the liquid sloshing into the cups, and I watched spilled water spread across the surface of the table.

Sweat was drying on my arms, tightening my skin. Tugging the puckered seams of my spandex shorts, I went to cheer Leyla and Gretchen at the finish line. I drew up beside Sam George who was whooping and waving his arms.

"Ms. Pont," he said. "I knew you were coming up behind me during the race."

"Yeah, I hung there for a while."

"I recognized your breathing."

I placed a hand on my throat, self-conscious. Sam had detected my own lime-scented fear, had heard it in the quick snap of my breath.

In my car on the way home, we all sat quiet, breathing heavily. The air conditioner was as loud as the tape deck. The Grateful Dead. Van Morrison: "I want to rock your gypsy soul, just like way back in the days of old." Bodies chilled. "Ta na na, ta na na na, she got diamonds on the soles of her shoe." Eyes were dry and sleepy. "I feeeeeel good, like I knew that I would, now." I turned the air conditioner down. Then a pert voice chirped, "This is a great mix, Ms. Pont."

I looked in the rearview mirror, surprised. Behind me, Leyla was sifting into a relaxed state. Salt from sweat was drying on her face, making it sparkle. In time with the music—Bob Marley—her chin bobbed just a bit. I could read her open eyes, her slightly parted lips. They said: *I am alive.*

Leyla had conquered fear.

I AM NOW AFRAID for another reason: Tom isn't at the spaghetti dinner. A senior, he is off visiting Bucknell, three hours away, with his parents. His presence is missed; he is a zealous eater who would have reveled in cannoli. Moreover, because of the timing of his interview, he might very well be unable to run the race tomorrow. Though, since the spring, the boys have been scheduled to run first, I plan to rearrange all the races around Tom's arrival, despite what the other coaches might say.

He was the first finisher from Moravian at the Blue Valley Farm Show with a time of eighteen minutes and forty-five seconds, respectable for a parched evening during preseason. He came to the first practice, wearing his Jean-Claude Van Damme T-shirt, fit. If he remains focused, he could shave a minute and a half off his time by the District XI race in late October and qualify for the state championship. A gentle guy with a Doric build and a black belt, he had learned, over the summer, to run with his entire body, even with his toes, his wrists, and his neck. I wondered, right from the start of preseason practices, who taught him that.

He told me. It was an afternoon practice, a second session with only a few of the top runners there: Tom, Dave, Mike, and Leyla. We drove to a path in Easton that follows the Lehigh River, a cool tunnel beneath a canopy of trees. There, we did an "out-and-back": twenty-five minutes out at a slow pace, then back at a quicker clip.

On the return run, Tom and I broke off from the rest. Knees high, we followed the soft curves of the river. Comfortable on the familiar path, comfortable moving swiftly, he turned to me and said, in a perfectly natural voice, "Are we going to do more speed work this year?"

"We're doing speed . . . right now . . . Tom." I heaved the words from my chest. Saliva on my lips rounded the edges of consonants.

"No, I mean *sprints.*"

"Yeah," I panted. "I did some . . . research. I have . . . some new drills."

"Good," Tom chatted. "One of the kung fu instructors said I needed to do more sprinting."

"Oh?"

"It was amazing. He watched me spar, and afterwards he asked me, 'Do you run?' When I said 'Yes,' he said that I should sprint more."

"He . . . doesn't know you run?"

"He just guessed."

"That's . . . amazing."

Couples walking dogs came toward us, smiling. A train whistle blew on the far side of the river. Tom's stride was consistent.

"We'll . . . sprint more. What's your goal?"

"To get into college," he laughed.

"No, really."

"Nineteen-thirty."

"You'll do . . . better than that," I squeaked. Picking up the pace, we rounded the hairpin turn that took us from the river to the parking lot. The path dipped down, then up. A waterfall roared to our right. Children, on pink and chrome bicycles, played behind the trees. The parking lot in sight, we broke into a full sprint. When we stopped, I doubled over, but Tom checked to see if the car was unlocked. There were snacks within.

A few days later, he beat his goal at the Blue Valley Farm Show. But what he said, I feared, was true: his real ambition was not to run but to get into college.

THE SPAGHETTI, cold now, forms a solid, rubbery mass in the colander on my sink; we've run out of bread; sauce leaks down the side of the trash can: I worry about first one thing, then the other, then the other. I have more general fears that play behind me like a sound track, accentuating dramatic moments, amplifying in times of ennui, fears like *This is too much for me.* I hear this in rain, in mugginess, when the runners become so spread out along a course I can't keep track of them all, and when, at Palmer Bike Path, the faster boys and I got lost.

Moist clouds hung low and loose so that the sun, through the haze, was a distant yellow speck. Leyla and Gretchen had frizzy hair and tired eyes. Water bottles felt heavy and clammy. Most folks were assigned to do an out-and-back, but the varsity boys—Sam George, Dave, Tom, Josh, and Oliver—were tackling the five-mile loop. I explained the route several times, but each time, I made no sense, even to myself.

Nevertheless, the team went out together. Then, after a mile, we were significantly spread out. The boys hung together at a comfortable gait.

"I smell pancakes," I said, nodding to suburban houses that flanked the path.

"Wild pancakes," said Sam, his voice pitched low. "Rabid pancakes. They're everywhere this time of the year."

We constructed the mythology of the Rabid Pancakes for the next mile, until we arrived at a fork. To the left, the road rose and curved in a direction far off from where we needed to go, while, to the right, the road followed a steady downhill that seemed to roll directly back to the parking lot where we had begun. We opened our strides, spread ourselves across two lanes, and headed confidently down the hill.

The pavement climbed steep inclines, narrowed, took two or three sharp curves. When we reached a gully, I admitted to the group, "This isn't the five-mile course, this is the *six*-mile course." Groans ensued, and our pace slowed significantly.

Abruptly, Sam stopped cold. We halted, too, circling him. Oliver and I came up to his chest. "This will take us back quicker," he said, pointing to a sign that said Bike Path, which marked a paved route down a steep slope.

"I don't know," I muttered, but, when the others trotted along after Sam, I followed his lead.

At the base of the hill, the Lehigh River thundered over a power-generating waterfall. We looked first upstream and then down. The river was wide and ominous. I never knew it could contain so much power.

"We're going to wind up in New Jersey," said Josh knowledgeably.

More groans ensued.

We walked up the hill and a little way along the hot road, eyeing yards for sprinklers. After a bit, we mustered our courage and finished the course at a steady, eight-minute-mile pace.

Beside a water fountain, sweat forming spots on his Bob Stores T-shirt, Dave said to me, "We could have run the six miles." Just by saying so, Dave revealed that he was able. The rest, however, were not. Minds that believe six miles is so much more than five can only run the five.

That mind-set was the rabid creature I feared most.

GRETCHEN AND LEYLA, smiling with pleasure, haul out the Tupperware. Gretchen's is filled with neat rows of peanut-butter brownie cupcakes which I have tasted before—in excess—so I reach for Leyla's monster cookies, speckled with M&M's, chips, and nuts. Although I haven't eaten the meal yet, I can have dessert first, I rationalize, because I am the cook.

Though spaghetti comes but once a season, I bake often. My cookies are not mere bribery; they are an instant celebration. Cure for our fear is the taste of our pleasure: Sam makes fun of me; I make fun of Oliver; Nimish and Rajeev play their private games for the public eye; Leyla frolics like a flower child. There is much to celebrate.

On my birthday, I baked chocolate-chip cookies and wrapped them into small foil bundles. Cut and collated pieces of paper contained clues for a scavenger hunt. These clues sent groups of runners all over campus, to classrooms, to my car, to the main offices where the college counselor was primed to give them a hard time before granting a reward. At each station, runners received letters: *C, O, O, K, I,* or *E.* The group that sprinted from site to site then back to me for further clues the quickest, piecing the word together letter by letter, would be victorious.

Josh, Gretchen, and Leyla got such an early lead that I had to tease them. I withheld a few clues, then hid from them in the bushes behind Snyder. Tom, with Rachel and Kate Webbink struggling behind, siphoned me out of those bushes for a clue.

Every group, even Bryan, Katie Hartman, and Sara, who were far behind, had every letter but *E.* Only one *E* existed, and I had it. As I saw the figures heading toward me, hungry, I bolted for Green Pond.

On the varsity soccer field, a wide-open expanse just above the pond, Josh materialized. He was after me so intensely that I was slightly frightened. I scrambled down the incline where the pond met the road, and I ducked down, knees bent, ready to run. When I saw Josh at the crest, his muscles tensed, his face set, I dashed along the road to the left. Then, when the crest became too high for him to see me, I immediately sprinted to the right. As fast as I could, I followed the road to the far side of the pond.

Josh hadn't given up, but he was tired from the game. I knew that if I just made it past the pond, I could hide behind the pump house. I smacked my sneakers along the path boldly, tearing past pricker bushes and snapping geese. Keeping my speed up despite my growing fatigue I ran . . . right into Sam George.

As he tagged me, I let out a groan.

"I knew exactly what you would do," said Sam, clutching his side. He straightened, and we walked across the fields to Snyder. "I was just waiting."

"Uh-huh. And I did exactly what you expected me to do, " I said. "I wanted you to win."

"Uh-huh."

Kate, Rachel, Tom, Holly, Josh, and the others fell in beside us as we made our way up. Sam explained his strategy a bit further to the envious losers, then regaled us with imitations of himself running at earlier stages of his career. "This is me as a freshman," he said, flailing arms and legs madly, but moving not at all. "This is last year's relay race." He ran in place, miming the spastic action of pulling a gingham sash over his head to pass it to the next leg of his three-man team. "Well," he laughed as we gathered in front of Snyder, "Now I've exhausted both of my jokes. It's lucky I'm going to graduate."

After rewarding the winning team with shiny packages, I thought about going for a run myself. But before I could move, Gretchen and Leyla appeared beside me. "Can we do this again?" they asked.

"Yeah, can we?" voices echoed.

"We'll do other things," I assured them. "Better things."

LIKE EAT SPAGHETTI. My kitchen is a Jackson Pollock of spaghetti strands. I throw out the matted mass of remaining spaghetti, then I scrape, stack, and wipe in the kitchen for a while. Finally, I dish myself up some salad, a little limp now from the dressing, and enter the living room. I hear the shutter of a camera, but otherwise the room is subdued. Everyone is sitting cross-legged on the floor, in configurations of two or three, knees touching, stray plates on laps scabbed with drying sauce. Only Sam George is, at times, gregarious. He is flirting with the new girl, Samantha, who just appeared today. I can't say that I blame him. Her gold-flecked hair is pulled tightly away from a creamy forehead. As he talks, her dark eyes do not blink.

Instead of joining a cluster, I listen to myself breathe. Sounds around me drift away as my lungs and heart make themselves known. The snap of valves, the gurgle of blood, the firing of synapses, and the flutter of air in my nostrils occur whether I am conscious of them or not—but there are moments in which I firmly believe that the systems are functioning more forcefully than others, fueled by external sources. Wedged between bodies, I sense my inner ear holding me balanced, my thumb's uncanny manual dexterity holding a fork, my cartilage holding me still in my crouched position. I know, though, that what truly holds me in this place is not my own body, but those around me.

They are all an attractive lot: slim muscles and wild hair. They may or may not run well tomorrow in the Lion Invitational, the huge race we host at the beginning of every season. Likewise, they may or may not run well in our eight dual meets, in the Bulldog or Solebury Invitationals, or in the final races for the district and the league championships. No one is bothering to speculate. Fear is no concern when pleasure is high. At times, winning matters solely; at other times, depending on how fine we believe ourselves to be, it matters not at all.

Suddenly, Sam George, Dave, and Samantha rise to go, planning to resume the party elsewhere.

"Take the leftovers with you," I insist.

"You can have them." The first rush of bodies leaves.

"Sleep!" I call after them. "We have a race tomorrow!"

Groans warp in the stairwell.

"Kate, get these cannolis out of here or I'll eat them all," I say.

After a few sheepish declines, Kate steps forward and reclaims them, but only after I agree to keep the cheese and fresh basil she brought.

On his way out, Sam Cohen hauls the bag of trash.

While I suds the empty pots, Gretchen wipes down the kitchen table with a yellow sponge. Leyla puts the chairs back in their places, knocking the wooden legs against her knees. The girls pack up their Tupperware containers and carry them, empty, back to their homes.

The first marathon runner, unnamed and so unacknowledged as a hero, carried the message of victory from the battle of Marathon to Athens in 490 B.C. The weight of that burden was so painful that he ran beyond himself and died. In the mythology I construct, though, I imagine him to be light. I see him naked, shining, letting the words of his message roll through his mind as if he were a player piano. He is running so freely that he feels the world is turning beneath him while he is suspended in air, enjoying the scenery as it passes. The arms pumping at his sides and the footsteps beneath him are not part of him. He forgets pain. He doesn't need to breathe. He is another element.

Sometime later tonight, Dave, Sam, Gretchen, Leyla, and the rest will aspire to that weightlessness but will fear that their own bodies might pull them down so that they cannot run, crawl, move.

Why, then, do they run?

2. Girls and Boys

Girls seldom see themselves. For that reason, one in a million girls, when told she is beautiful, really believes it. Gretchen should. She has tiny fingers and a quick chin, a spackling of nutmeg freckles, and a trusting gaze that turns inward when she runs. There, I imagine, is where she seeks her beauty. Though she is new to racing, having played field hockey in the past, she has made running a mode of self-definition. In her imagination, being first across the finish line gilds her, encrusts her with jewels, makes her a goddess in the eyes of all who watch her.

In reality, Gretchen's pace, in practices, places her second on the team. But today, our first race, Gretchen has the chance for newfound plumage as long as she can endure the pressure of being watched.

In the speckled shadows in front of the school before our first race, the Lion Invitational, Gretchen's mocha skin, still tanned from summer, is gold on the surface and sapphire in the hollow beneath her arms. She is wearing a loose white tank top with a white sports bra underneath. She is alone, here much earlier than the rest of her team, eager to help, to preempt the pain of the race by taking pleasure in the idea of it. The clippers I hand her to trim the course are longer than her arms, but she snips them skillfully in the air.

We walk the 3.1-mile cross country course—standard length for high school competition—along the soccer field and around the pond, following the lines of white I spray-painted earlier that morning, snapping at sumac and prickers, pulling up the limp, green branches tangled in the undergrowth, then tossing them behind the tree line. She kicks aside rocks; I scrape at goose dung with the treads of my running shoes.

After we set the foot-high orange cones in place at the tricky turns on the course, we walk slowly back to the front of the school. As today is the Friday before the start of the school year, I ask her about the classes she will take, the English she scorns and the French she loves.

Bluntly, she brings the subject around to the race. "What should I do?" she asks, her eyes brown disks, thickly lashed.

"Think about the race one mile at a time," I say. I describe the terrain of the first mile: slightly downhill, then slightly uphill. "Really focus on the second mile. New runners lose lots of time there." I encourage her to think about the race in three stages. "Find your sprint when you come through the gate by the soccer field." As we wade through the shaggy grass of the campus, our arms swing and knees lift in time. Though she is listening to me in earnest, looking at me full, I know that coaching, at this point, has no bearing on the race. All her hope is in the swing of her arms, the lift of her knees, her belief in herself, and time: if preseason was enough time, she will, in this race, while the watch ticks, become who she wants to be.

All her fear, though, has nothing to do with the Poe-like tick of the watch; time does not watch the way people do, judging, snickering, looking away. Like all athletes, she knows she will be watched, but she can only speculate on how she will be seen.

Because crowds have gathered around the school, Gretchen drops away like a dream. Teams are spilling out of yellow school buses; spectators are slamming the doors of minivans. The other runners on Gretchen's team have arrived and are starting to warm up—stretching and jogging—leaving their warm-up suits in an orgiastic pile.

I divide tasks for the finish line: official timekeeper, scorekeeper, someone to give a Popsicle stick with a number on it to each of the finishers. I clear the two stopwatches around my neck and watch the athletic director load blanks into the starting gun.

Then the East Stroudsburg girls step up to the line, their thighs curving like rivers. Northwestern Lehigh, Pocono Mountain, Bangor, Saucon Valley, and Stroudsburg crowd in. The girls are tall; the muscles in their necks and arms wink with inhalations, exhalations. They look forward, their eyes carefully prepping the rest of their bodies for the cycles of pain that will turn like gristmills for the next twenty or so minutes.

I arrange all of them—fifty-seven total—by team. The Moravian girls shiver together, backs to the course. I have to grasp both of Gretchen's tangerine-like biceps to turn her around, pull her up to the front of the group, and place her along the line with our top runner, Ann, and the leaders from the other teams. Gretchen's fine jawline is a knife; her walnut eyes flicker. Though the row of runners is alternately tall and short, with a spice rack of hair colors, there is a uniformity. The way their sports bras tug at their chests, they are greyhounds in gates, wanting to spring free.

Girls crowd behind their top runners, chests tight against backs, not wanting to waste a single step when the race begins. Kristy, our girls' captain, has nudged up to Gretchen's shoulder and is instructing some of the younger girls to do the same. Flush against the tree line, they press into Gretchen, hoping she will pull them to the front of the pack.

As the gun goes off, I thumb the buttons on my watches hard. Time, for me, stops. Runners funneling into the narrow space behind the Ballards' house become immobile. Coaches, necks heavy with stopwatches, arms heavy with clipboards and notebooks, head off for mile and two-mile marks. Fans scatter. Nearly everyone has fled the starting line. All is quiet. In my imagination, I see runners alongside the field hockey field, by the softball backstop, behind the pond. I picture Gretchen out front, seeing her as she wishes to be seen, thinking that my positive thoughts will transport her.

Mrs. Worsley, Gretchen's mother, is at my side, rousing me. In her face are Gretchen's fine eyes, thumbnail nose, and clustered freckles. "Where do we go?" she asks, all eagerness and intensity. She places lashlike fingers on my arm.

To the mile mark. We dash off to the double white line I drew where grass bleeds to pavement. My gait is serious; I try to pull along those who are racing. As I move, I imagine Gretchen on the road, over the log, by the soccer field. At the one-mile mark, I stop. I ready my stopwatch to collect mile splits. I envision Gretchen in front of the headmaster's house, by the gate, up the grass . . . but suddenly there are two runners fighting for first place, and neither is Gretchen.

"Keep it up, Holly!" "Go, Pocono Mountain!" "All right, Laura!"

The first two runners, from Pocono Mountain and Stroudsburg, run the first mile in just over six minutes and show no signs of faltering. At that pace, they should finish the race in less than twenty minutes, impressive times for female runners this early in the season. They are both long women, whittled at the extremities, but the Pocono Mountain girl reaches with her legs, as if testing the air in front of her for its temperature.

She is beautiful because she is winning.

As more runners pass, coaches and spectators shout first names, last names, team names, team colors. They instruct, they cajole, they praise.

Mrs. Worsley calls out, "Pick up your knees, Gretchen!"

"Use your arms!" I shout.

She does not glance our way.

Our lead runner, Ann, passes the mile mark in 7:23, Gretchen close behind at 7:30. Her eyes are focused on the back of a runner in front of her, avoiding the gaze of the watchers. Though her face looks stunned, her breathing is smooth.

The quantity of runners passing thins. Kristy appears in 7:40, Leyla 7:42, and the remainder of our varsity girls in slightly more than eight minutes.

"I'm so nervous," says Mrs. Worsley, clutching my wrist. The weight of her wedding band presses into my skin. "You would think I was running." She rests her palm on her chest to measure its pounding. The nylon of her azure wind suit sighs.

After Katie passes by in 8:28, I run-walk with Mrs. Worsley to the two-mile mark. The girl from Pocono Mountain beats us there. I wonder if she will break the course record: 19:36. I hope she doesn't.

She doesn't, but she enters the flagged finish chute at 19:48. The runner from Stroudsburg takes an impressive second, then Northwestern Lehigh and East Stroudsburg fill in a number of places.

But the race isn't over and will not be until all fifty-seven girls cross the line. Contained within every race are a myriad of other races, against the person beside you, in front of you, just behind you. Before the race begins, you resolve to lean your chest across the finish line first, to raise a hand to percussive applause, to lower your head for the weighty medal, but inside the race, perspective changes and ambition shrinks; you simply want to be faster than somebody, anybody, else. Though only the first five runners on a team count in the final score—points allotted by place, first earning one point, second, two points, and so on—the slower runners compete with equal fervor, frantically struggling to avoid last place, that dwarfish kingdom of ugliness and shame.

With a tenth of a mile left, Gretchen is fighting to be number one on the Moravian Academy team. As Ann passes through the gate by the soccer field and comes up the grassy slope to the finish line, Gretchen is just behind her, fists white, sprinting as hard as she can. Her lips are a tight *O*. Her back is erect. She is gaining ground on Ann but, more importantly, on an idea of herself. Gretchen's gaze leashes itself to the finish line. Her arms and legs are working so hard she looks as if her body will split in two.

She runs out of time, though. After Ann falls across the line, Gretchen blows in behind her like a leaf. She leans into the multicolored flags of the chute. When she receives her numbered Popsicle stick, she doesn't look at it.

Ann finishes twenty-fourth, with a time of 24:42. Gretchen is five seconds behind her in twenty-fifth place, and Kristy seven seconds behind that in twenty-sixth. Not far behind is Leyla in twenty-ninth place.

Five minutes is too long a time between the top runner and our first. Moravian Academy loses to everyone but Saucon Valley. But those statistics are irrelevant to the girls, some of whom met personal goals and some of whom, like Gretchen, didn't. Kristy moves from Gretchen to Leyla to Ann, dispersing hugs that no amount of sweat can deter. The comfort of bodies gives them some hope, reminds them that they have two months of training before they face these teams again.

After the hugs have passed away, Gretchen stands apart, hiding herself in the grape-colored shadows of trees. Speckles of sunlight flit across her face like thin, heatless flames before the fuel ignites them in a sudden burst.

When the boys' and the junior varsity races are over and the other teams are leaving, I pick up an empty Gatorade jug. Gretchen gathers skins of orange quarters from the grass. Others are pulling on their sweatpants. "We'll have practice tomorrow," I announce.

"I can't be there," says Ann.

I look at Gretchen to see if she is relieved that she will be the fastest girl at practice, but she is intent on plucking chewed fruit peels and piling them in her palm. Her face, full of mauve light from the late afternoon sun, could be the center of a flower. But she will not know that until she wins.

IN THE MORNING, I part with my *New York Times* and head for school and practice. I walk through grass syrupy with dew. Along the way, past field and garden, I seek signs in nature for a good practice, a better day, a killer race next week at the Solebury School, a school in our league. The sun is silver, the goose dung fresh; some roses on the trellis are dying, some just opening. Which signs apply? With what Rosetta stone can I read them? The sun is in my eyes, blinding me.

"Did you hear about Princess Diana?" Mrs. Worsley greets me. Her children, Gretchen and her younger brother, flank her.

"What?"

"She was in a horrible car accident." She is genuinely grieving. She wraps her arms around the shoulders of her children and pulls them to her. "Those poor little boys. Who's going to love those little boys?"

Imagining the risky ventures of driving and of motherhood, I search myself for a response but can only nod.

I don't know how to read this sign.

I am pleased, though, that Gretchen, Dave, Sam George, and Samantha have gathered in the parking lot. In the past, it was hard to know who would show for the optional weekend practices, particularly this one, on Labor Day weekend; families usually retreat for beaches and picnics. I feel lucky to have two boys and two girls. That balance, I decide, is a good sign.

Samantha and the others seem to agree. Their mood is high. As we stretch in the parking lot behind Walter

Hall, Gretchen laughs at Sam and Dave's jokes and listens attentively to Samantha's stories about life in Maine where she lived before she moved to Bethlehem a week ago. We are drenched in sunshine as we start our run to the community college.

Samantha, who, because she is so new to the team, didn't run in the Lion Invitational, is keeping up easily. Her stride is loose; her arms are away from her body; she holds her hands open rather than clenched. Gretchen, too, seems to be having no problem. She keeps her arms at a more acute angle, and her knuckles are pronounced. Running beside her along the pine trees lining the college, I ask for her peanut-butter brownie cupcake recipe.

"That's my grandmother's," she says.

"Then maybe I should leave it for your family archives."

"No, no! She'd want you to have it."

And I'm one recipe richer.

Further on, by the cornfield, I am bantering with Sam and Dave. I instruct them where to go in order to cover four miles. As we are about to cross the road, I look back to signal to Gretchen. She isn't there.

Going back, I find her behind a tree. She is holding her knee, limping. "My foot," she moans.

I come up beside her and put a hand on her shoulder. "Put pressure on it," I say. She complies, poised like a bird, good leg tucked up. "Is it a sharp pain or more like a bruise?"

"It's not bad," she says, turning a sad face to me. "I can run."

"What kind of a pain is it?" I insist.

She circles her arms to balance herself. "A bruise."

"Let's walk."

I talk about pain, about its ebb and flow, about how sometimes you must give in to it.

Gretchen picks up her knees a bit. "I think it's OK," she says. "Let's start running." Not only because of her large eyes, her swift nose, and her mocha skin, but also because she wants so badly to run, she is more beautiful than ever. Picking up her pace, she views only the uneven grass in front of her, while her pretty feet kick swiftly behind.

Though I know she is lying, that she is, in fact, in some amount of pain, I am relieved. Neither she nor I want her to be really injured.

Despite Gretchen's inclination to speed up, to catch up, I keep our pace slow. I know she shouldn't force it.

Meeting up again with Sam, Dave, and Samantha as they curve around on their loop, we run the three-quarters of a mile home in a neat line. Samantha erupts in a brisk sprint at the end. The rest of us struggle to stay with her. After we stop, we are winded and sweaty.

In front of Walter Hall, breathing, the sweat on our arms evaporating in the warm air, I can see changes in them. Dave seems more aggressive, desirous of speed;

Samantha grateful to be running again. Gretchen, most of all, seems sadder and wiser, recognizing her need for running after finding herself on the brink of injury. She turns her ankle this way and that, daintily, to measure the pain sneezing inside her bones against her desire.

I AM TALKING to Mrs. Worsley on the phone. There is swelling in Gretchen's ankle,.

"She's my kid," says Mrs. Worsley. "I can't help but worry."

"She needs to take a couple days off," I say.

"She's afraid she's going to get slower."

"It'll be worse if she aggravates the injury."

"Is she going to be ready for the next race?"

"She will if she rests."

"She wants," her voice breaks, "this so badly."

"We all want it for her," I assure her.

"What we want for her doesn't matter."

"I know."

IT IS SEPTEMBER 13 and Gretchen is on the bus that is transporting us to the Solebury School for their invitational race, twisting her ankle, first this way, then that, listening for cracks and tears. In the back of the bus, the older kids sit, listening to their Walkmen or sleeping. In the middle seats, the younger ones do homework, geometry and biology books on their laps, cleft knees rubbing against each other in the aisles. Gretchen is between the middle and the back, half of the time reading her French, the other half staring out the window. Up front, I am jostled around behind the driver, motion sick, trying to avoid my own nervous eyes in the rearview mirror.

After opening the window by my seat and the one behind, I sink deep within myself, wondering about time. An hour and fifteen minutes to get there; two hours to run three races and present awards; an hour and fifteen minutes back. But those times, in the context of the season, are irrelevant. Only arms, high knees, and desire affect runners. In the past thirteen days, I hope, my runners took time off their times. I'm fearful about Gretchen's ankle, and I know she is, too.

As we drive, we pass schools, churches, dairy bars, and old stone barns. This is unknown terrain. I try to read a book. The country roads dip, pitching us up and back. I put my book away. We pass restaurants, pastures, and 7-Elevens. The numbers assigned to roads—412 South, 212 East, 611 South, 202 North—seem mathematically improbable. My stomach gurgles.

After we've been on the road an hour, the bus driver interrupts my discomfort to ask, "Do you know how to get there?"

Gretchen closes her French book and looks up, eyebrows arched.

I shuffle through my clipboard and find a booklet of

directions that our school prints up for parents. I read road names aloud from the smudged photocopy. The directions take a risky turn that leads us on a course down, then up the Delaware River on 32 North. As we drive slowly through New Hope, a tourist town, some of the younger girls call out, "Can we go shopping?" Gretchen rolls her eyes.

I look at my watch: we're running out of time. It is 2:45 and the race starts at 3:00.

We pass housing developments, railroad stations, country inns, and several intersections.

When we reach Phillips Mill Road—the last road— a cheer rises from the back of the bus. The bus strains to climb the narrow and steep macadam. I feel as if I am carrying the bus on my back and its weight will split my body in two.

At five minutes to three, the bus pants into the Solebury School. Leaping up, I instruct the driver to let me out. The door flaps open like a tongue. I jump from the top step and hit the ground hard. As I run to halt the first race, I feel small and slow.

Although the quiet of their fields isn't promising, I sprint to the Solebury coach and hold my side as she tells me, "We started the boys' race at three." I look at my watch. It says three. I breathe heavily into her face. She holds up her own watch. It reads 3:05.

"We'll start the girls' race at three ten."

I charge back to the bus.

Running and walking, our arms tight up against our chests, I quickly try to explain the course to the girls, most of whom have never been here before. Kristy helps me out. As Ann couldn't come, Gretchen is especially attentive. She walks beside me, listening closemouthed because she might need to blaze the trail for the others. The course, I tell her, closes off quickly into a wooded path; it goes through hills, hits pavement, wraps around the school buildings in a way that is trickier than it looks.

I am describing and talking strategy too quickly, though. My talking is not the same as walking the course.

Gretchen shucks her jacket and wind pants; her lashes brush her apricot cheeks. Gaze still down, she finds the starting line. As the crowd of runners quiets, I touch her shoulder. Her eyes open wide as the world.

The gun goes off before they can really stretch. Brown, blue, and red uniforms vanish into the woods. I jog over to where the mile mark should be but find no official line. At the top of the long down hill that passes a mile mark I estimate, figures appear. They run down the hill, gaining definition. A few girls from Episcopal and one from the George School pass, then Samantha. Though she is running with tight arms, her mile split seems fast. I don't read it off to her; I am afraid the time is wrong and she will gain false confidence.

Mrs. Worsley joins me, nervously pacing around me while I check my stopwatch.

"Gretchen seems OK," I say.

"This means everything to her."

"I know."

When Gretchen passes, a minute behind Samantha, her motions are stiff. She seems to be listing. She glances over at her mother and me to see how we are seeing her. Before I can mold her gaze with a smile and a nod, she looks away.

Mrs. Worsley reaches her hands out to Gretchen's vanishing figure. "I just wish I could do something," she groans.

I imagine what she would do, if she could: set Gretchen's splintering ankle, conjure a wave of wind that would blow Gretchen effortlessly to the finish line, sooth Gretchen's prickling mind.

When Gretchen passes us again, Mrs. Worsley runs beside her a few steps, telling her how great she looks. Mrs. Worsley's blue warm-up suit shimmers.

Samantha finishes in sixth place with a time of 21:54, Leyla eleventh with a time of 23:44. Gretchen, thirteenth, twenty-one seconds behind Leyla, is favoring her foot. Though her time, 24:05, is better than that of her previous race, she is so frightened she will not look at me.

"Ice and ibuprofen when you get home," I order her. She nods tightly, chin down, eyes cloaked, keeping her face empty of emotion.

She stays at my side as I study the girls' results on

my clipboard. Though Episcopal beat us squarely, we lost to the George School by a mere two points.

"If we had time to stretch," I reassure her, "we would have beaten the George School. Maybe even Episcopal."

But that is not the race she cares about.

Gretchen walks toward the bus with her mother, her head still lowered, emotions tumbling from her like autumn leaves. Gretchen is murmuring her dismay with coming in third on the team. Her mother praises, nearly chants, "You'll be second, next time; you'll be first." They embrace, then Gretchen mounts the bus.

Just before I get on, Mrs. Worsley pulls me aside. "We have to make her believe in herself." I search myself for a response but can only nod. I step aboard the bus.

It drones off into the dusk.

In fields, lightning bugs flicker among feeding deer.

While the rest of the team snacks on cookies and peanut-butter brownies, Gretchen shows no interest. Instead, she snuggles into her seat, holding her ankle, slim and smooth despite the pulsing pain within.

Thetis, nymph, was the beautiful mother of Achilles. Her love gave Achilles his mythic strength. Holding him by the heel, she dipped his body into the River Styx, laminating with immortality all but his heel. In her maternal zeal to make him strong, she succeeded, really, in localizing his weakness.

Mrs. Worsley has given Gretchen beauty and talent;

she encourages Gretchen to speak impeccable French and to dress, like the French, impeccably. I wonder, can her love make Gretchen see herself?

I think of Princess Diana and other mothers: love, at best, is a risky venture.

DON'T BE FOOLED; simultaneity seldom makes for parallel experiences. For the Lion Invitational, Sam George arrives just as Gretchen and I finish trimming the course, but all he shares with Gretchen are space and time.

"Ms. Pont!" his voice booms, deep and bold.

Gretchen and I, walking by the rose garden, holding clippers and a few extra cones, cut our conversation short and give all our attention to Sam. We can't help ourselves.

"Everyone's looking for you, Ms. Pont."

"Even you, Sam?" I tease.

"*Especially* me." He tilts his face charmingly and gestures with his arms fawningly. His body is long and pale, like almond slivers, and he keeps it in motion, fully in control of its changing symmetries. He has developed this choreography through a lifetime of training: at seven months, he played the Baby Jesus before a sold-out crowd. Since then, he has not stopped acting. He is used to being watched. Early on, someone told him, convincingly, that he was handsome. Unlike Gretchen, he does not doubt himself.

His dark features are Chinese brushstrokes on his pale face. Why should he doubt himself?

While Gretchen and I laugh, Sam goes through one of his two running shticks: imitating himself as a freshman. He exaggerates his motions more and more until we are exhausted in our laughing. Still gasping, I go off to greet the visiting teams, and Sam seeks others to entertain.

Boys, more often than not, are judged by what they do. Sam George does what his father, Bill, does: he acts, pantomimes, projects, quotes, gesticulates, orates, clenches his fists, darkly broods, evokes giggles and gut-busting laughter; he sucks out the marrow of life. At times, though, Sam is much better than his father: stronger, racier, more streamlined, with a keener sense of timing. At once, they seem to come from the same instant and from different centuries; they seem to share everything and nothing.

To share in Sam's senior year of high school, Sam's captaincy, Bill joined us during preseason for morning runs. They framed the group. Wearing cutoff denim shorts, Bill ran, noiseless and serene, with the back of the pack, far away from Sam, who presided over the front in black T-shirts and worn bandannas, boisterously chronicling his summer at the Governor's School for the Arts. Their forms were different: Mr. George leaning forward, Sam upright; Mr. George swinging his arms against his lower ribs, Sam holding his fists high and crossing them in front of his sternum. Mr. George's eyes narrowed like a falcon's; Sam's widened like an ostrich's. But before practice and after, they fell together into the deft, practiced braiding of words and gestures that was their visual manifestation of love.

I invited Bill to the spaghetti dinner the night before the Lion Invitational.

"I can't," he said, his sinewy voice wistful. "I'm touring."

"You're going to miss the season?"

"I'll be gone six weeks." He pulled his voice from his abdomen in weighty skeins. "I should be back by districts."

"Good. Sam will need your cheering."

"Sam can take care of himself," he assured me. "He's his own man now." In his sadness, Bill looked away. I wondered what Sam would do without him.

AT THE LION INVITATIONAL, now, the first home race of his senior year, of his captaincy, Sam is alone. When I send the boys on their warm-up run, he guides them confidently, much taller than the rest, and they fan out in a chevron behind him.

The crowd seems quieter without Bill George's grandiose cheering, but Sam, bent on racing, doesn't notice. He's leading warm-ups, his teammates around him in a perfect circle. When he pulls his arm across his chest, the others do so; when he reaches for heaven, the others do so; when he forgets the next stretch, he does not doubt his ability to remember, nor do the others. Why should they? "That's right," he says, reaching for the earth.

The girls' race is over. Sixty-two boys—from East Stroudsburg, Stroudsburg, Pocono Mountain, Saucon Valley, Northwestern Lehigh, and Pius—now crowd the line, thin, bare shoulders riddled with sunspots. In their loose tanks, they are even more uniform than the girls. Only Sam, in black socks, really stands out. He and a few other runners do stride-outs, erupting from the line like freed greyhounds, legs thin and acutely muscled. Though the others return to the line in sheepish jogs, Sam is upright, noble.

When the gun sounds, I don't hesitate: I am off to the mile mark, alone. As I run, I imagine Sam intimidating the others with his height, his demeanor, elbowing past runners one by one with well-paced drama. Thinking of Sam, I cannot hear the other coaches chattering until two boys appear, fighting for first place. Neither one is Sam. Their coaches step forward to cheer.

"Keep it up, Rich!" "Go, Stroudsburg!" "All right, Dan!"

The first two runners, from East Stroudsburg and Stroudsburg, run the first mile in just over five minutes.

They are both high-cheekboned men, pointy-jointed, but the East Stroudsburg runner reaches to the sky with his knees.

Close to each other, our top three runners come up the grassy hillock. Tom, in seventeenth place, crosses the mile mark at 5:59. His shoulders are forward, his feet turned out. Dave sneaks by on cat feet in 6:11 with Sam George three seconds behind. I call out, "Use your arms, Sam!" As he passes the crowd at the mile mark, Sam's legs are turning smoothly, but his torso is too tight. His eyes are blank; he follows no one. The noise of the fans wakens him, though. His eyes ignite, his temples pulse, and his body opens.

Behind him, Bryan and Sam Cohen complete the mile in just under seven minutes. Because they are all toward the middle of the pack, their faces are shy and apologetic. Their bodies will not cooperate with their minds' desire.

Moving quickly, I make it to the two-mile mark before the East Stroudsburg runner crosses. I am slightly afraid that he will break the course record: 16:32.

He doesn't. With a time of 17:05, he isn't really close, and he falls against the flags of the chute after receiving his first-place Popsicle stick. The runner from Stroudsburg takes second, then Pocono Mountain and Saucon Valley fill in a number of spots. Tom finishes in 19:25, Dave in 19:38, Sam George in 20:44.

Two minutes and twenty seconds is too long a time between the top runner and our first; Moravian Academy's boys lose to everyone but Pius.

At that statistic, however, Sam George simply shrugs. A Dixie cup of Gatorade in his hand, he is looking over my shoulder at his time.

"Not bad," he says, "For not having run at all this summer."

"That's a great first race," I agree.

"It felt really good. I'll be three minutes faster by the end of the season."

"Of course," I say, believing him completely.

Before I give winning teams and individuals their medals, Sam and Dave tell me they *need* to leave; they are planning to see *L.A. Confidential.*

"You *need* to run and pick up the cones," I say.

"I'll do it," says Gretchen.

"Everyone *needs to,*" I insist. "It's a cool-down run."

I glare at Sam, but he won't change his mind. His father was right: Sam is his own man.

A GOLD STICKER emblazoned with NEGATIVELAND adorns the back of Sam's car.

"I like the bumper sticker," I say.

"It's a band," says Sam, and quotes some lyrics.

It is Labor Day weekend, and Sam, Dave, and Samantha are unsuccessfully empathizing with Mrs.

Worsley's sadness over the death of Princess Diana. This sun-drenched morning is too warm to think about sons needing parents. They seem relieved that I've changed the subject. Sam and Dave quote more songs by Negativeland while we stretch.

Then, running in the sand and broken glass along the narrow road toward the community college, hopping over roadkill and trash, Dave and Sam paraphrase *L.A. Confidential*. They are running quickly, happily, letting their light banter keep them aloft.

"We should make it to states," says Sam.

"We need to work hard these next couple of weeks," I warn, trying not to sound negative.

Sam loosens his arms, self-conscious about his form.

"I'll be under twenty minutes next race."

"To make it to states, you'll need a seventeen thirty at Lehigh," I say.

"I love Lehigh's course."

"It's harder than our home course."

"I know what I need to do," he nods, affirming his belief in himself.

Again, I believe him.

Gretchen having twisted her ankle, I lose Sam for a mile of the run, then rejoin him for the end. We turn into the driveway behind the school, then open up a full sprint to the front.

There, bent over and clutching our knees, I see

changes in them. Dave seems doubtful, wishing he weren't so winded after four miles; Samantha seems doubtful, wishing she had arrived sooner so she could have raced yesterday; Gretchen seems doubtful, wishing she had somehow avoided what she fears is a real injury.

Sam is Sam, though, unchanged. He walks off with Samantha and Dave, talking about coffee shops, bands, and films, planning the fun he will have the rest of the day, the rest of the weekend. As his itinerary grows more vivid, his tone escalates. Samantha and Dave listen to him mesmerized, convinced that Sam will show them the time of their lives.

I don't doubt that he will.

FOURTEEN DAYS LATER, we are competing at the Solebury School. Because our boys missed the varsity race, they will run with the junior varsity. While the girls' varsity race is under way, Sam leads the boys through a warm-up run on the first part of the Solebury course. They see the pricker bushes, divots, and unmarked turns. When Sam lines up with Dave, Tom, and the other varsity boys for the junior varsity race, he chuckles. He is relieved and excited to have no competition. His race isn't a race; it's a search for time. He is unintimidated. Time is no real competition.

Without competition, though, time remains an abstraction. At the mile mark, Dave is knotted, Tom slanted, Sam huddled. Without a race, they cannot really run. Their first-mile splits, even without accurate measurement, are zany in their speed; their second miles are lugubrious. In his third mile, Sam looks like Dr. Zhivago in Siberia.

Dave first in 19:19, Tom next in 19:25, then Sam in 20:22, all stagger across the finish line, limbs quivering. Though Dave's time improved from the previous race, all of them are shaken. They believe that time has done nothing for them.

"We didn't have time," says Sam angrily. "We got here so late."

"You can't think of this as a real race," I say. "You didn't have any real competition."

Sam looks stricken. "We would have gotten killed!"

"I don't think that's true."

Looking over the results on my clipboard, I match up our boys' times from the junior varsity race with those from the varsity race. I count on my fingers. Sam, Dave, and the others would have come in second, behind Episcopal and ahead of our traditional rival, Girard.

"Actually," I say, "You might have won."

Sam looks over my shoulder at my clipboard. "We *would* have won," Sam mutters, dissolving any semblance of fear. "We just needed time."

"You need a race that's really a race," I say. "You haven't had that yet. You weren't in shape for the first one, and we weren't on time for this one."

"When we are, we'll win," says Sam.

I thoroughly believe him. Happily, we cheer as Samantha receives a medal for her race, and we all celebrate on the bus ride home from Solebury. With the sounds of torn tinfoil and cracking cans of Gatorade, the party begins. The girls sing, swaying their shoulders in unison. Sam cracks jokes, quoting from *The Simpsons* and obscure movies. I drink from a can and study my clipboard in the dimming September light. Sam's right: the numbers I see show nothing but promise.

Sam, alone, sneaks through the dark aisle and joins me in the front of the bus. He folds his legs up against the seat in front of us as if they were onion stalks.

"Do you have a Walkman?" he asks.

"Of course." I untangle it from my bag. He sees I am listening to Ani DiFranco. He puts the headphones on, listens to half a song, then slides the spongy pads down to his neck, the music still playing.

"I'm going to see her next Friday in New York." He swings his fists in a tight circle.

"But Sam, the Bulldog Invitational is on Saturday. That's an important race."

"I can do it."

"Sam, you can't do everything."

He frowns. The shadow of his father, traveling and acting, passes before his eyes: miming and brooding; sucking the marrow of life.

"I can do it," he insists. "I'll sleep on the bus."

"You're taking the bus? You won't get home till four in the morning! You need a good night of sleep."

"I need to see Ani."

"I should just drive you. I'll go out and have a nice dinner."

His lips thin suggestively. "I think I can get you a ticket."

And it's agreed: I will join in on Sam's fun and get him to bed on time, to boot.

SO, I IMAGINE the week. We will have our practices: long distance, middle distance, speed. The day before the race, we will do a couple of laps. That night, Sam will lead me into the unmeasurable excitement of his world. I will drive him and his friends to New York City in my Volvo. The girls will smell of patchouli oil. Their dyed hair will be pinned back with baby phat barrettes. Sam will wear black. My car will be full of gas, music, and oil-colored bags of chips. With the girls in the middle seat and Sam at shotgun, he, his friends, and I will sing along with Ani, Negativeland, and all the other music we love as we ride toward the lights of the city.

But all the while I will ask myself, does Sam want his

father to be here? Has he wanted his father here all along to watch his races, to affirm his experience, to shout Sam's name loud enough to make the clouds buckle, to make Sam feel as if he were a god?

Zeus had many sons, daughters, and acolytes, some heroes, some gods. Cadmus, though, a mere mortal, Zeus loved best of all, so much so that they were partners in a series of adventures: killing monsters, challenging whole armies, sowing life into dead ground with dragons' teeth, and founding the walled city of Thebes, the home of Oedipus and Antigone.

When Cadmus became king of Thebes, Zeus and he parted ways. Cadmus had a city to rule, and Zeus a cosmos. Being king, though, felt flat to Cadmus. It lacked drama. He would rather have been slaying mythic beasts while Zeus smiled with complicitous approval on Cadmus's bravery and prowess.

Sam and Gretchen both know that the stopwatch doesn't watch a runner the way people do: with awe and affection; with disgust and dismay. What they both have to learn over the next month and a half is that the stopwatch sees things as they truly are. Only if they woo the watch not with the beauty but with the integrity of their bodies—the smooth muscles of the stomach and buttocks, the endocrine glands, the alveoli, the platelets—will they be the winners they wish to be.

In order to do so, they must forget fathers, mothers, other boys and girls. In that respect, Gretchen and Sam are no different, though their experiences have diverged and will continue to do so along the separate running trails that boys and girls take.

3. Perfection

ractice seems to make perfect, once it's over. Then, with the pain of the practice evaporated from muscle and joint, Leyla more than anyone else on the team feels cleansed, strong, and slightly amnesiac. She takes the lead in the cool-down run, her body scuffing the just-mown grass like a fallen leaf, thinking she can do the whole practice all over again, just wishing she had the time.

A cross country practice at the high school level can last anywhere from forty-five minutes to two hours. Each type of practice—long slow distance, middle distance, and speed work—serves a purpose. Before the Bulldog Invitational this Saturday at Northern Lehigh High School, we will do one of each. Inside all three, even the shortest or most structured, there is an ebb and flow in a runner's comfort level. Though Leyla, because of a strong heart, is best at the distance workouts, at irregular intervals she floats, while at other times she succumbs to gravity's pull.

To magnify the floating and minimize the sluggishness, amnesia is essential: forget the memory of that which occured before; forget the pressure of that which awaits. At the moment, Leyla has a lot to forget. Because her mother is sick, the care of her five younger siblings has, in large part, fallen to her. As Leyla is tiny, not much more than ninety pounds, some of her younger brothers are bigger than she.

So Leyla climbs inside a workout as if it were another world with different clothing, customs, and expectations. It is almost as if, when running, she snips and trims away everything except the slip of her body.

I wonder how long she can keep running this way.

In the cafeteria on Monday, Leyla rushes up to me. "I'm not sure I can make it to practice," she says uneasily.

"Do what you have to do."

"I want to be there," she says emphatically.

"I know that, Leyla."

Later, in the locker room, Leyla sheds her black knit dress and dons a red T-shirt and black soccer shorts. After she folds the dress and tucks it into her bag, the transformation is complete. She changes from a woman to a girl. Her oat-colored hair curls around her face.

"I'm glad you're here," I say when the team gathers outside the school. "Today will be fun."

"I have to come," she says.

"Don't come because you feel like you have to."

"It's not that. It's my mother," Leyla says simply. "That's why I have to run."

On our warm-up run, while the rest of the team jabbers aimlessly, Leyla keeps quietly to herself until we round the pond and reach the far side of the campus. She noiselessly takes her place in the warm-up circle but steps forward to listen attentively to my description of the workout.

I have set up cones around the lacrosse field for 200-meter runs. We will do six. In the September sunshine, the field shimmers like water. The sky is pale silver, the sunlight white. Before she starts running, Leyla is already beginning to glow from the heat around her, the heat within. Blood, risen to the surface of her skin, paints her face in aboriginal badges. If the pale Leyla of the morning still resides in her, it would take some mining to find it.

I divide the team into groups. Leyla is in the second group, mixed with girls and boys. She could squeak through the knees of some of the boys. At regular intervals, I shout, *"Go!"* and legs gallop around the cones. Through round after round, Leyla sustains a steady pace, with just a little slumping in the deadly fourth one. Her form is perfect: shoulders back, legs extending from hips, elbows at waist level. Both nature, practice, and desire conceived that perfection.

Between our fifth and sixth sprints, we pause. Breathing is heavy, murky, like French horns. Leyla thrusts her knuckles into her lower back and massages. The sweat on her face glistens in the sun.

"This is the best thing I've ever done," she says, a little giddy.

"Leyla, I think you're delirious."

"No, really. This is so much fun."

I look around. "Does anyone have any water? Leyla's a little dehydrated."

Leyla runs the last 200 meters perfectly. As she bends over, catching her breath, she is radiantly smiling.

As we begin our cool-down run, Leyla sees Oliver coming over the hill. When I tell Sam George that I'm going to run practice with Oliver and that he should lead the rest of the team into school, Leyla eyes both Oliver and me enviously.

The workout over, she wants to run again but now needs to confront her life.

———

TUESDAY MORNING, I see Leyla before school begins. She is with a group of freshmen and sophomores, heavy with backpacks, who are complaining about their homework. She steps away to talk to me. She is uncertain, once again, whether or not she will be at practice. Lilac half-moons swing beneath her eyes.

"Leyla, do what you have to do."

"I'll run at home."

"I'm not concerned about that. You just look so tired."

"I'm not tired," she says, then laughs. "Except in the normal sense. I'm just worried."

When the bell rings for school to begin, Leyla brightens, entering that world.

And Leyla finds herself, later, at practice, spritely in her green turtleneck and blue cotton shorts.

For our long-distance workout today, we load vehicles and caravan through the narrow streets of Freemansburg to a path along the Lehigh River. With Gretchen and Holly, Leyla is folded into the back of my station wagon. In the rearview mirror, I see their heads close, giggling.

We park along the river, cross over to the other side where a well-worn path cuts between the river and the canal. After stretching on a dusty strip beneath an overpass, I explain the workout: twenty minutes out for the top runners, fifteen for junior varsity, at an easy clip.

Everyone should be able to converse. At twenty minutes, turn around and return faster. The less time it takes to get back, the better.

The river flickers umber and tin. The leaves wave. A fisherman smokes a cigar. Little kids on bikes race and wipe out. On the other side of the river, a train passes, cranky and smoky. Conversation goes from school to music to films, then back to school. As we pass beneath a low-hanging branch, everyone jumps to reach it.

At twenty minutes, the dense group of eleven runners at the front of the pack turns in a variety of manners: K-turns, point turns, loops around trees. Their bodies, though, alter in unison: legs extend, arms reach, shoulders tighten, smiles erase.

A hush falls. Sounds of breathing mount, like Stravinsky woodwinds signaling a change in mood. Five minutes pass, then the crucial ten. At this midway point, some runners break their pace, falling behind, but those up front relax into it, thrilled by the speed.

Leyla is right there. She is keeping up with Tom. Her lips are moist and her neck muscles twist, but she exhibits neither fear nor pain. She is running without emotion; she has pared herself down to nothing and is simply running.

That is desire: allowing for nothing beside that which it craves.

Leyla can't keep it up. Tom pulls away from her and

finishes in 18:25, but Leyla churns out a good sprint at the end and is only thirty seconds behind him.

"That felt good," says Leyla. Sweat fastens her curls to her cheeks. She brushes them off. Though her breath is greedy for air and her shoulders are slightly shaking, she is examining the smooth dirt path, wishing she could again vanish up it.

As we stand in the parking lot, passing around jugs of Gatorade and Dixie cups, wiping sweat on the sleeves of our shirts, Leyla's arms are crossed. She waves a Dixie cup of Gatorade away.

She pulls me aside. While the rest of the team teases and gossips, Leyla whispers, in earnest, "I have to make it back to school for the bus."

"We'll make it."

My assurances mean nothing; until our cars pull into the back of the school, Leyla is wrapped in anxiety. She is holding on to herself so tightly I fear she will never be able to unravel.

But as she runs to catch her bus, she cuts through the wind like a song.

"Keep it up, Leyla," I whisper.

"I DON'T THINK I can make it to practice," she says on Wednesday. Thistle shadows circle her eyes. Her navy cardigan hangs from her shoulders, exposing a flinty collarbone.

"You know how I feel: do what you have to do."

And, happily, she is there, in a thermal shirt and nubby socks.

I explain the workout: it is middle distance with a little speed and a lot of competition. I set up an elaborate series of concentric loops, each one bigger than the next, with four stations in each loop. I then divide the team into groups of four. The teams will run each loop as a relay. The group that wins the most number of loops gets a prize. For the lucky—the fastest—I have bags of Swedish Fish and bottles of Frost Gatorade waiting in Walter Hall. The first lap is a sprint; we all will see one another run. For the last three loops, we will diffuse into the campus.

As part of the first leg of a four-person team, I am up against Leyla, Kristy, and Tom. Though we all cheer madly for the other members of our teams, Tom's takes an early lead.

We chatter as we wait for the other runners to get to their stations, speculating on the upcoming Bulldog Invitational.

"I think we'll do well," says Leyla.

"It's a big race," warns Kristy.

"Bigger than this," I say.

"I wish races were like practices," says Leyla.

"In what way?"

"Fun."

Kristy is about to tell Leyla she's crazy, but I interupt. *"Go!"* I shout. Within a few steps, we are sprinting as hard as we can, running like rickshaw drivers on the balls of our feet so that we hold on to our places. As the distances lengthen, Leyla gets farther and farther away from Tom. On the third loop, she is ten yards behind his heel. Nevertheless, she pushes herself as hard as she can.

The third leg complete, the four of us stand close, watching the other runners dart like dragonflies through campus. Rachel, the last leg of Tom's team, finishes first. Tom's face trembles; he is trying not to trumpet his pleasure in winning.

"Good job!" calls out Leyla as the other runners find the finish.

The last loop, the full 1.3 miles that span the perimeter of the campus, takes a few minutes to set up. Leyla enjoys the quiet of waiting. But when I again shout, *"Go!"*, our feet are thunderous on the pavement. We know this is the end of it. After Leyla, Tom, Kristy, and I pass off to our next runners, we jog back to the starting line to witness the end, eager to win.

"You're gonna win it, Tom," says Leyla.

Shyly, he smothers a smile.

Kristy lets out a whoop. From over the hill beside the pond, her teammate Dave emerges all alone.

"Go, Dave!" cheers Leyla. She springs up and down on her toes, waving her fists.

Dave hardly uses his arms. His stride, though, is

economical, with a swift churning of his legs from the hinge of his hip. As we watch him, we all feel a hybrid of awe and affection.

"Great job!" calls out Leyla as the rest of the runners tumble to a halt in front of us.

Everyone crowding around me, I check the tallies: Dave, Kristy, Vinayak, and Sara win. Dave's face quivers; he is incredulous about winning.

As they are awarded their Gatorade and Swedish Fish, we all cheer, Leyla the loudest. Though it is getting dark, Leyla has plenty of time before her bus leaves, so she talks with some of the other girls about running a few more laps.

"Just one," I insist. "We don't want to overdo it. Remember, we have a race on Saturday."

When they return after their single lap, Leyla appears content. The rings around her eyes seem ethereal, pretty; her general tiredness has folded into a sense of calm. She walks toward her bus easily, unworried.

Practice makes perfect because practice changes us, sloughs off the dead cells to replenish them with fresh ones. Although there is a science to training, the theory only works if it successfully meshes with life. Leyla is emerging from the week stronger: better able to run, better able to live.

When Lucy Pevenskie in *The Lion, the Witch, and the Wardrobe* went into the wardrobe to hide herself from the world, she found another one. What happened in Narnia—magic, tea, mythic creatures, and triumph— made her emergence back to the real world easier. But she always longed to return, and, in the end, did forever. And that was perfection, as far as she was concerned.

Leyla, too, might run forever and find that to be perfection, but I suspect she would not choose it, if offered. Rather, she would leave that perfection to practice and go home to be with her family.

As with skin, there are layers of reality, compressed, that we use to cloak our selves. Leyla has exposed many of those strata. Somewhere in that epidermis, though, is a reality for which practice may or may not have prepared her and which Leyla has still to touch: another race.

SIMULTANEITY sometimes makes for parallel experiences. The world jostles itself, shifting energy and debris, until it finds balance. Just as Leyla walks away from me in the cafeteria on Monday, I turn and find Oliver.

He is sitting at a round table with a cluster of freshmen and sophomore girls, making strange shapes with his vanilla pudding. An approving laugh erupts from his entourage.

As it settles, Oliver looks up from his sculpture and calls to me. "Ms. Pont!" He leaps from his chair and rushes to where I am sitting, bumping a few chair backs, elbows, and passersby along the way. "I have an after-school detention," he reports. "I can't be at practice. Oh, well." He exaggerates a sigh.

"No problem," I say. "I'll run practice with you afterward."

"Doh!" he brings his fists across his abdomen in Homer Simpson fashion.

"Why do you have a detention?" I make my voice sound stern. "History?"

"Chemistry," he groans. "I forgot to turn in a lab."

"Forgot?"

"It's *almost* done!"

"Almost . . . ," I begin, but his entourage calls him away.

Oliver is a good boy who always skirts the periphery of trouble. He is a bright boy who gets so-so grades. He is a handsome, blue-eyed boy who, he tells me cheerfully, has been dumped by girls fifteen minutes into a relationship. His older brother, Winston, was the best runner Moravian Academy ever had.

Although the rest of us worry that Oliver is not making correct choices, is not living up to his potential, Oliver remains blithe, untroubled. His carefree attitude worries us all the more. We wonder how long he can keep running his life this way.

Another round of laughter echoes through the cafeteria, Oliver's table its source. He has matriculated from pudding to spoons, plunging their cupped ends into cubes of solid food, then building a second story atop them with pieces of burnt toast. He could get into trouble for his crude architecture, but, when the bell rings, he whisks away the evidence to the dish room. Then he scurries to class where he will, no doubt, earn from teachers and classmates praise, appreciative laughter, and a scolding or two.

I shake my head, wondering about this absence of desire.

THE SCHOOL DAY HAS ENDED. Without Oliver, we take our warm-up run to the lacrosse field at the far end of campus. I divide the team into groups for sprints. Though practice runs efficiently, we are, without Oliver, missing some mischief and some magic.

As the team is beginning its cool-down run, Oliver appears like Puck, ready to play any role commanded. The shadows under his chin and his arms are teal, his pale skin pink in the afternoon sun. To join us, he is running faster than his body appears able.

He comes right up to my side, unafraid, like the actor he is, of talking near my face. I say to Sam George, "Lead everybody back to school, I've got to run with Oliver." Oliver falls in beside me, and we bifurcate from the group, heading toward the science labs at the corner of campus.

As Oliver and I do a warm-up lap, I tease him, "Oliver, you need to leave those freshman girls alone and find an older woman."

"Aargh," he says. "Ye wouldn't say things like that if ye knew I was a Viking."

Oliver constructs the mythology of his Viking persona for a mile, adding to it a few of his *Simpsons* shticks and an imitation of his former French teacher, until we arrive back at the lacrosse field and the cones. There, we pause by the first one. Abruptly, Oliver shouts, *"Ga!"*, erupting into his run. *Ga?* Confused, I pause before taking off, and Oliver gains several steps on me. Nevertheless, I catch up and pass him.

When people run, their bodies, more or less, conform to the same choreography: the arms swing, the legs lift. Only in those most basic motions are Oliver and I alike. I run with muscles, and Oliver runs with heart. By the fourth time around, he is beating me soundly.

We finish our cool-down run in front of the school and stand for a moment, our hands on our hips. Around us is a Cezanne world of washed blues and spruces. Oliver reaches out for a wiry coil of my hair and tugs. "Curly . . . straight," he says in a cartoonish voice. He tugs again. "Curly . . . straight." Though I swat his hands away, I am laughing at all his jokes simultaneously.

As Oliver needs to catch his bus, he tosses out one final imitation of his French teacher for a closing chuckle. I am tempted to burst into applause. Oliver is conscious of what works. He is stronger than I know, but not stronger than he knows. Underscoring his caprice, I am learning, is a lacy matrix of control. He might do better in the Bulldog Invitational than I originally suspected.

IN THE CAFETERIA, Tuesday, as I am pouring my morning coffee, Oliver scampers up to me. His throat is ringed with a row of string necklaces, black and taupe and lime green.

"Where's your tie, Oliver?" I chide.

He reaches into several pockets before fishing it out. "Well, at least I have *that,*" he says. His blue eyes grow mournful. "I forgot my sneakers."

"What size are you?"

"I can't wear yours!"

I sip my coffee. "Not mine. But someone in this school has to have your size."

"*Doh!*" He dashes off to find friends and sneakers and to discover which of his homework assignments he forgot to do.

After school, Oliver is wearing his sneakers. "I forgot that I had them," he says, his lips drooping sheepishly.

For our long-distance workout, we load—circus-clown-like—thirty runners into a few vehicles. The cars, low-slung with human cargo, squeal to a path along the Lehigh River. As it is a favorite workout for many, the mood is cheery. Besides, Oliver is in my car, riding shotgun, fiddling with dials.

Under a highway overpass by the river, we circle up to stretch. Sam George leads us through a series of contortions, then instructs us to get down on our stomachs. Arms and legs extended and taut, we pull and tighten our abdomens. Sam pretends to be swimming the breaststroke—sweeping motions of the arms, frog kicks of the legs—and musters a laugh.

Oliver picks up on it. "Swim for the fishies," he says, snatching at invisible creatures in the dirt and weeds. Though his hands come up empty, his eyes appear to truly see them.

After I break the team into two groups for either a twenty or a fifteen minute out-and-back, the twenty-minute group starts out, restraining urges to run fast. Oliver should be among them, but he settles back with some slower runners to continue an involving conversation. After several minutes I look back and I can just see him and his merry band appear and disappear behind golden boughs, thick trunks, and rope swings. After several more minutes I glance back again and the full leaves of the chestnut trees are masking his group completely.

"Twenty minutes!" I shout.

On the way back, after a minute or so, the front runners come across Oliver. He is solitary; he is serious. For the next seventeen minutes, no words escape his lips. He is wholly involved in the part of the practice that really matters.

Sustaining an aggressive stride, Oliver finishes not far behind Tom. Though the rest of the runners drift to the cars to drink Gatorade, Oliver waits for his friends. At that moment, those friends are the part of his life that really matters.

I wonder why we worry about Oliver so; twice, in thirty-eight minutes, he made the correct choice.

Before we drive home, bickering occurs and seats switch. Dave is riding shotgun; Oliver is in the back. Dave makes a face then fishes from beneath his thighs a single Swedish Fish, red, in plastic wrapping.

"Finders keepers," I say.

He promptly eats it.

When we are back at school, Oliver inquires about the Swedish Fish he accidentally misplaced in the front seat of my car. When I tell him its sad fate, he is outraged. "You better go to Switzerland and get me another one."

"Sweden," I say. *"Sweden."*

He puts a finger to his lips. *"Doh!"*

"MS. PONT," SAYS OLIVER when I see him on Thursday before chapel. "I don't know if I can come to practice."

"Forgot your sneakers?"

"No. I just have so much homework. History is killing me. I wish I was a ninth grader again."

"You didn't worry about your homework then, why are you worried about it now?"

"*Doh!*"

HISTORY DOES NOT KILL OLIVER; he is ready, after school, for a road trip. It is two days before we run the Bulldog Invitational, and we drive forty minutes through slate-mining country to Northern Lehigh High School, the host of the invitational, in order to learn the terrain of their course. As we are tapering for the race, easing runs to give muscles a rest, this is a fact-finding mission rather than a practice. It is an important one, too; because the Northern Lehigh course twists around the school in a zany, convoluted manner, knowledge prevents a bungled turn, disqualification. With twenty teams participating in this race, every tiny advantage is essential.

Maps in hands, we jog the first half mile of the course, following well-marked lines. The entire course has been closely cropped. It is a two-yard-wide strip that is an inch shorter than the grass around it. At some points, different-colored arrows point in both directions. A few of the new girls shake their heads, confused.

We pause near a line of trees to stretch, then we continue along the course at a faster pace, checking maps and discussing the terrain as we go. It is a day with a high wind that makes it difficult to talk. I worry that important observations are going uncommunicated.

For the first mile and a half, Oliver scurries along with the top runners, listening and helping with the map. By the time we reach the two-mile mark, though, which follows a tree line up a nasty hill, he has vanished. I look behind, but the buildings of the school obscure the view. No Oliver.

The course takes a hairpin turn around an elementary school, leads down a hill, cuts through trees, and ends at a track. A few of the top runners wait with me outside the fence that surrounds the track, but most drive the forty minutes back to school. Still no Oliver.

"Where is he?" I exclaim, craning my neck to peer through the chain link, through the mesh of trees, up the hill, to latch my eyes on Oliver and pull him to me. He will be one of our top five runners; he needs to master this course. Moreover, he needs to gas up on desire. I cross, sharklike, behind the fence. "Where is he?" I say again. Leyla and Gretchen, arms akimbo, regard me with quiet fear.

After ten minutes, I see Oliver with Sara and Rachel, walking through the thicket and down the incline where the path feeds into the fenced-in track.

He approaches me, anticipating my questioning. "They would have gotten lost."

He is absolutely right, and I am wholly grateful. How well he must know this course suddenly occurs to me: the year before, he ran wisely, well-paced, in the freshman race at the Bulldog Invitational. Despite the quantity and quality of competition, he kept his head and finished with an impressive time.

Rachel and Sara have been lost before during practices. Because they are new runners trying to find their legs, it would be devastating for them to be lost during a race, especially this one, at which hundreds of spectators, with camera lenses and stopwatches poised, affirm that the winners have won and the losers lost.

Oliver had the sensitivity to know all that and so walked when he should have run, knowing the walking really mattered.

As ever, there is wisdom in his folly.

In Shakespeare's plays, the fool's role is to point out the foolishness of others. Touchstone, Shakespeare's most lovable fool, partakes in the foolishness to expose it most fully.

Touchstone exposes the folly of love, an easy target. Oliver, though, is more philosophical. He critiques our notions of perfection by draping them over himself at times, then discarding them as quickly. Oliver runs, often very well, but winning is inconsequential. If it happens, it will, no doubt, be accidental.

Whoever set the standards—devised the grading

system for schools, drew the tapes across finish lines—did not anticipate Oliver and does not have methods with which to accurately measure or adequately reward him. Nor did they, those arbiters of perfection, anticipate Leyla, who runs well because so many things, to her, are of consequence. Like Puck, Touchstone, Ariel, and other characters, Oliver and Leyla are "such stuff as dreams are made on": spirit. And with what process or stopwatch is spirit measured?

4. Sam I Am, I Am, I Am

"What's *Liberty* doing here?" I ask Sam George after I jump from bus to pavement at Northern Lehigh High School on Saturday morning. His little blue car, emblazoned with the Negativeland sticker, is parked tightly beside the yellow school bus. Side by side, we gaze at Northern Lehigh's track. Around its periphery, several dozen Liberty High School runners, male and female, in fanatically matching red, white, and blue T-shirts, stenciled jackets, wind pants, headbands, and sunglasses stretch their long, lean legs in a loose, rhythmic gallop. Murky steam rises from the tarred surface so that the Liberty runners appear to be crossing the River Styx.

"Aren't they always here?" Sam asks, untroubled. He minces a granola bar between his fine teeth, peeling the paper wrapper back as if it were a banana.

"No," I say. "This is the Colonial League. Liberty's gonna kick everyone's ass."

Samantha has joined us. Though she knows nothing of Liberty, the Colonial League, or the names of other local schools and conferences, she eyes the Liberty runners appreciatively, knowing winners when she sees them.

An independent school of 250 students, Moravian Academy is in the Penn-Jersey League, a collection of small private schools primarily in the Philadelphia area, rather than the Colonial League, which consists of the larger public schools in the area surrounding Moravian Academy. Our appearance at this race is always a risky venture. Once, a few years ago, our boys' team picked up a second-place trophy; some individual boys have, over the years, earned medals for placing in the top ten. No Moravian girl, however, has walked to the winners' table at the end of the race for a bit of metal, a squall of applause, a halo of fame. This year, with Dave, Tom, Sam George, and Samantha healthy and running well, I had aspirations for some piece of hardware or another.

As Sam reaches into the bus for a second granola bar, I shoo at his hand.

I had not anticipated Liberty. The Liberty runners, out of everyone's league, with some of the best athletes in the state and often in the country, will make all the competitors look as if they are walking.

Gretchen, Leyla, and Samantha, because they are new to the course, want to walk it again despite our trip here two days ago. We leave behind Sam George and the others to spread out coolers, blankets, sweatshirts, and bags of snacks in the crosshatched shade beneath the metal bleachers, confident about their knowledge of the course.

Starting to walk, I continue to quietly grouse about the presence of Liberty. Samantha, without knowing the specifics, hears my tone of voice. Because she understands that the level of competition is scalding, she keeps quiet as we walk.

I point at a double white line that hugs an orange cone. "You gotta watch this turn, Samantha."

Her smile brightens suddenly and brilliantly as a maple leaf: I am the only one who calls her by her full name. To the rest—and to herself—she is simply Sam. But she doesn't mind that I have sculpted her another identity. In fact, she incorporates it neatly.

"I wish there were more hills," she says dreamily, thinking of her old home in Maine.

"Don't worry. You'll gain some time on that hill in the last mile."

Imagining the harsh, elongated uphill beside the elementary school that we ran the other day, she smiles again. She has an extraordinarily beautiful smile, if only because she smiles about everything, even the steepest of hills.

We blaze the course in the blackstrap September heat. A few of the younger boys follow along, but Sam George and his buddies on the varsity are out of sight, lounging in the shade, sipping Gatorade. The girls run and walk, testing their breathing. For some, lungs are having difficulty chewing the thick air. Samantha, though, is relaxed. She eyes the cones and the lines gently, knowingly, as if she could draw them in and make them a part of herself. Her neck and deltoids are tight as cords of red licorice; she is running in her mind already.

As we face the first uphill of the course, just past the one-mile mark, I try to focus on Samantha—and, at moments, successfully do so—but I am beside myself in the most literal sense of the expression: I am two people, one calm, focused, the other outraged. Liberty shouldn't be at this race, my mind blathers. Because there is only one number one position, it shouldn't be allotted before the race begins.

Neverthless, there is a third me, one who grudgingly accepts my fate.

Samantha, though, is open to possibility. After walking the course, she veers for the bus to wait in its cool, plastic-scented interior, to sip water, to think about what she can and cannot do. The course has many twists, turns, and obstacles, especially with the presence of Liberty, but she keeps her worries to herself, her wide eyes focused, her full lips closed, her two braids straight, waiting for the truth to play itself out.

I check out the scene in the gathering place beneath the bleachers where Sam George, in protean voices and motions, is telling stories, jokes, lies, and other truths.

Why do Sam George and Samantha see this situation so differently?

All Sams are not alike.

Three Sams populate this team, two male and one female. At least once per practice, usually on our warm-up runs when we are stretched out in a motley parade along the sunburnt playing fields, someone calls out "Sam!" meaning one or the other; all three respond, and the rest of us laugh at the confusion. We could rename them, for practicality's sake, but each Sam is, to the marrow, Sam. They carve out an identity because of the name and despite it. None of them is singular in their Samness; contained, each within themselves, are many more Sams, each with uncannily Sam-like qualities. And then, within those, are still more Sams . . . and so on. Being a Sam is a complicated matter.

To be a Sam means a great deal not only to the Sams but also to the rest of us, who know that Sams are a little more complex than your average Oliver, Leyla, or Coach Pont.

On this team, then, there are an unlimited number of Sams, both male and female. Each Sam, though, vies to be the real one, the sole Sam, in a competition that is like a race. And as in any race, there is only one number one position. Be it boy or girl, flamboyant actor or earnest girl with paintbrushes for hair, there can be only one Sam.

To that great race for identity, an ultramarathon run every minute of life, we lost one Sam already, three days ago.

SAM COHEN'S SHIRT and tie were orange shot through with silver and black, perfectly matching. He and I were sitting at a round table in the cafeteria, looking at his college essays. They were spread before us like an open poker hand, waiting for the ante. I felt I owed him my time, my teaching, and more; a few days before, he taught me an invaluable lesson.

During the warm-up run at the beginning of practice, Sam Cohen fell in beside me, his lean frame arcing forward, his Sussman Brothers T-shirt waving like a sail.

"How's it goin', Sam?" I asked, adopting the exaggerated inflections he and his friends use.

His smile crowded his eyes, then he grew serious. "Ms. Pont," he said, "there's something I wanted to talk to you about."

"Shoot," I said.

"That day during preseason, when I said I had to be at orientation, and you said I had to be at practice? I think you should have let me make my own decision."

My head split open with shame. I had trouble keeping myself running.

"You're absolutely right," I said quietly.

"I'm not criticizing, I'm just saying."

"I know." My shoulders were cold. "I shouldn't have forced you."

"I just thought I should say something to you."

"It's good that you did. Thank you," I said simply, because I couldn't tell him how aware of myself he had made me, how much he had changed me.

Sam and I fell away from each other, running without talking, each feeling how hard learning could be.

We came together again at a sticky table in the school's dining room, and I felt slightly daunted to climb back in the teacher's seat. Sam's essays swam before me. He believed that I had the power to give him what he most desired—an acceptance letter from the University of Pennsylvania—and his faith was terrifying. I was afraid I would fail him again.

My pen worked its way down the paper. Because

the voices of Sam and his friends chattered around me, I felt, once again, like two people: one cool, mechanical, and the other wholly overwhelmed. Punching my thumbs into my temples, I returned to the first sentence of the essay I was attempting to read, unsure about the meaning of a single word.

"Kirsh!" Sam bellowed across the room. Sam's best friend, Keith Kirshner, approached, his voice booming a response. More bodies crowded around, Clayton and Scott, loosing in-jokes with every exhalation. Though I pulled the paper closer to my face, I couldn't help but glance up at the waxy face of the cafeteria clock.

"Ms. Pont," I heard Sam's voice demand, "aren't you done with that essay?"

I jerked my head up, guilty, and began to apologize to the faces watching me, but Sam simply grinned, nodding happily because he had so successfully teased me. Kirsh patted Sam's shoulder, his meaty hand closing over Sam's sharp collarbone, and left. With cheerful farewells, Clayton and Scott followed.

The table quieter, I finished wading through the essay. Relieved, slightly bleary, I gave Sam my impression of it, pointing out a number of changes. With my felt-tipped pen I scribbled notes in the margin.

Sam's face darkened like a wildflower at dusk. His close-set eyes pleaded. His long fingers, tight with nerves, fiddled with the edge of his essay.

"Can I call you tonight if I don't understand a comment?"

"Of course."

"Can you look at the changes tomorrow? I need to get this in the mail by Friday."

"Of course."

"And Ms. Pont," he paused, mouth parted, waiting for words.

I tingled with a jigger of anxiety. Because Sam trained little over the summer, he was quite susceptible to injury.

"I don't know if I can run on Saturday."

"You're not injured?" I squeaked.

"No. I need to go visit Penn."

I felt the cleansing of relief. "It's your decision, Sam."

Again, I was divided: I was pleased to be able to say it, but I was not so pleased with the reality of the situation. Though Bryan and Josh were riding the Tilt-a-Whirl of chronic injury—fractures, strains, and stray bolts of pain—the loss of a Sam represented the loss of many. Sam, though, gathering together his essays, looked more troubled than I. He was divided in profound ways. He looked around for Kirsh, Clayton, and Scott, but he had shooed them away. The papers and books under his arm made him list.

Often we speak of losing or gaining time, through traffic jams, short cuts, or other tricks and foibles of time management. Really, though, we never lose or gain time. Rather, we lose ourselves to it. The danger of losing to the watch is its effect on desire: desire becomes diluted, slowly begins to dissipate into the ash heap of compromise.

Time is a storm that forces us to jettison innocence.

WITHOUT SAM COHEN, now, at the Bulldog Invitational, the varsity boys set out for their warm-up run, cutting diagonally across a football field toward the back of the school. Sam George leads, his arms set tightly at right angles. His legs seem to come up to his shoulders. He has been on the team four years, has run the Bulldog Invitational in all the years of its existence. His face is carved with the longitudinal shadows of his age. His cheekbones and his stature speak: he senses that his time has come to emerge as the triumphant Sam, the sole Sam.

The morning sunshine has solidified into opaque moisture. Dank clouds hang low. More teams have arrived, some expected, speckled with faces familiar from our first race. Others, though, are wholly unexpected— Wilson and Panther Valley flank Liberty, striding from the starting line in their warm-up runs, looking tensile and formidable in shimmering uniforms.

Over the loudspeaker, an echoing voice announces the start of the boys' varsity race. The air smells of deep-fried foods. The starting line, fifty yards long, is crowded with 117 uniforms and barking coaches. I stand behind our seven varsity boys, giving last-minute advice. Sam's uniform hangs from him like soggy towels. One at a time, he shakes his legs.

The gun sounds. Cheers explode. The cannon fire of running feet tapers and is lost.

The runners reappear at the one-mile mark. Sam is deep in the first third of the runners. He towers over those around him, his elbows crossing their ears. His time is strong; at six minutes, he is just ten seconds behind Tom. I scribble numbers on my clipboard, hopeful and thrilled at the thought that Sam will beat his own time from the previous race by as much as a minute. And, if he can do that today, what of next week? and the next? I greedily watch his back, narrow as an elm leaf, legs light as kendo sticks. I am jealous of the building around which he darts; it can watch him longer than I.

A mile later, just as he is about to mount the hill to the elementary school, I call out, eagerly, "Go, Sam! You can do it!"

But he can't hear me, can scarcely hear or see anything outside himself. He is placing his feet, willy-nilly, in blurry puddles of air. There is a war within him—an angel and a devil telling him alternately what he can and cannot do. As he begins the dreadful climb up the hill, he is listening to both sides, terror-stricken.

The boys' race is ending. Four Liberty runners pick

up spots in the first eleven places. The posse of Liberty coaches, in their headlight sunglasses, shouts fanatically.

When Sam finally emerges through the trees, on his way to the track and the finish line, he is pale but conscious. The war within him has ended, for a time, but his feet strike the ground hard. There is, for him, no winner.

Sam grinds out a wild finish, dramatic and tragic as Lear. After he falls through the chute, he stumbles up to me on Frankenstein limbs.

"Your time was your best so far," I say gently, reaching up to touch his shoulder. "Twenty oh two."

His tight body gives a little to gravity. "I can do this," he says, thinking of the next race, but, for the first time, he seems genuinely doubtful. To doubt means, in its Latin origins, *dubitare,* to waver between two points. So he and I walk together in silence. I wonder which Sam will speak, the fearful or the hopeful, and I wonder with what ears I will listen.

The gun sounds for the girls' race, and 113 pairs of smaller, quieter feet fly off in search of time. Ann is not among them; she did not appear for the race, and I fear she has quit the team. When I position myself at the one-mile mark again, watch in hand, I am watchful for Samantha.

At one mile, Samantha, too, is deep in the first third of the runners. She is small and compact, but her arms are open as if she is welcoming the coming miles. Her time is impressive, 6:18. I jot numbers on my clipboard, suspecting that she will soundly beat her own time from the previous race. And, if she can do that today, what of next week? and the next?

Samantha sustains her pace through the second mile, then moves onward toward the hill. Though there is no change in the expression on her face, her shoulders fan out a little wider.

I cannot know what is happening to her on that hill—what skirmishes within herself she is winning and losing—but I try to watch her with senses other than sight, to hear her footfalls in the sound of my own breathing.

She emerges through the trees even sooner than I could have anticipated, her open arms in full swing.

The girls' race is ending. Four Liberty runners pick up spots in the first seventeen places.

And Samantha is just behind them, number eighteen with a time of 21:43, faster than her race at Solebury. When she springs free from the finish chute, I hug her shoulders. Her skin is hot against mine, and her smile flashes. Though no medal, clapping hands, or haloes await her, she is in one way victorious: her finish is more impressive than that of any Moravian Academy girl before her.

Together, eating apples, Sam and Samantha watch Liberty clean up in the junior varsity race, each through very different eyes.

I place my hands on their shoulders. "Let's leave," I say. "We don't need to watch Liberty cart off all the hardware."

On the way home, emotions whip through us all, carving us to pieces. Sam George, on his own in his own car, is already two people, I imagine—who he is and who he aspires to be. His great consolation is this: he still has time in our dual meets over the next few weeks to fuse the sides of Sam together.

ON MONDAY, another race looming in two days against the Perkiomen School, I decide it's time to play a game. I set up an old favorite called fox and hound, the storyline of which has a strange inversion: a rabid fox chases the hounds that should, in a normal scenario, be pursuing it. When the fox catches its prey, the victims become rabid and turn on their fellow hounds. We carry the extended chases throughout the campus, disrupting, at times, soccer and field hockey practices. Those athletes, lined up for tightly choreographed drills around neon cones, watch us jealously as we parade our freedom.

Everyone is excited to play but me; Sam Cohen is not at practice because he has a doctor's appointment.

Nevertheless, I give the team strips of white cloth to tie around themselves to signify their status as hound, except Tom, who is set to be the rabid fox. When he gives us three minutes to scatter, I bolt off with Samantha, who has never played the game before, to hide. As we make our way to the far side of the soccer field, I ask her about herself.

"I have a boyfriend in Israel," she freely volunteers.

"When is he going to be home?"

"Three months."

"That's a long time," I say.

She shrugs, more involved in her running than in the concept of time. Neither duration nor distance bothers her. We walk a bit by the soccer field, run again, glancing over our shoulders for predators, and walk some more, moving away from each other then back together in parabolic patterns.

"I feel guilty not running," she says.

We resume a jog, keeping our eyes open for Tom or any hounds turned rabid. When we see Oliver, we begin to sprint, but he waves his banded arm to calm us.

Samantha then scurries off to the far side of the school, possessed with the desire to run. By myself, I see chases, like strings of meteors, flicker on the other side of campus, along the tallow cornfield behind the pond, beneath the disbelieving gaze of the soccer coach, through the autumn trees, just yellow at the crown. Distant shouts of pursued and pursuers pop and trill.

Then, I, too, am chased and caught by Katie and Mike near the parking lot. We walk, laughing breathlessly, to the front of the school where others have gathered.

Practice over, breathing relaxed, Samantha and I walk side by side into the school.

"My mom can't come till late," she chatters. "My brother is playing football, and she has to go get him."

"Why don't you come have dinner with me?" I ask.

"That's OK. I'll just get some homework done."

"I wish you'd come."

She is easily pursuaded. When we walk into my apartment, it is steamy with the smells of rosemary and vinegar. All day, a beef stew has been brewing. I dish up peppery bowls, set with nuggets of gold and carnelian, picking out a bay leaf.

"What's in here?" she asks, smiling.

I rattle off the various meats and vegetables.

"How did you think of *that*?"

As we eat, we giggle over the haphazard nature of my cooking.

Samantha is happy to linger, to talk of running, boyfriends, and the social mores of Moravian Academy. She seems untroubled that it's late, that she has a ways to go through the purplish fall night to get to her home, that she has homework in all her subjects. She has not so much as glanced at the kitchen clock, its arms opening and closing to symbolize the time. Symbols may represent time, but Samantha does not impart them with time's reality.

When her mother arrives, Samantha is as happy to

go as she was to stay, springing to her feet as if starting up a hill.

The idea of time fills us all with trepidation, except when the time is good. Then, time is an occasion, on its way to becoming a treasured memory; then, it is never lost. Samantha converts all times—the waiting and the motion—into good ones. Hence her perpetual smile.

Later that night, Sam Cohen calls me, not about his essays. A doctor found something wrong with his hip; he can't run for three weeks. Those three weeks become a symbol for me of time's control, but I am too frightened to truly contemplate that symbol's reality for the boys' team.

ON WEDNESDAY, the morning of the Perkiomen race, I buy a bag of bagels and some mango juice to ward off dehydration. Though Perkiomen is a team not actually in our league but close to it, I want to take precautions to ensure a victory.

During second period I tote the bagels into the cafeteria where Sam George, Sam Cohen, and Dave are waiting while soccer players watch enviously, jockeying for position to see if there are any leftovers.

"I don't know if I should have one," says Sam Cohen, his manner gentlemanly, "seeing as I'm not running today."

"Eat it," I insist, "I'll put you to work at the finish line."

He does; Sam George sips juice; other runners wander through between classes and dig their fists into the paper bag. They walk away, plump bagels between tight knuckles, munching happily.

When school lets out we step into a world canopied in blue. The air smells of lemons. The red, green, and orange flags of the chute that I set up earlier in the day wave festively. Nimish and Rajeev, Oliver and Leyla, Samantha and Sam are chasing each other through the just-mown grass, giddy—almost delirious—with being alive.

When Perkiomen arrives, a long stream of boys troops off their bus flanking one girl, a brooding, muscular young woman with pudding-colored hair.

"They have no girls' team," I mutter, incredulous.

"So we win," says Samantha.

I collect myself. "Let's see your time," I say, mustering sternness. "That's what you'll be racing against."

But I demand information from the Perkiomen coach.

"She'll score as a boy," says the coach, confidently. As I walk along with the Perkiomen team, I see how their boys defer to her, questioning her in hushed tones, maintaining a distance as she stretches. She is, indeed, a boy and a girl.

When I report the information to Samantha, she smiles fully, her eyes drawing down to meet her upturned lips. "I'll beat her," she says.

In the citrus air of the fall afternoon, the boys and girls line up together for a single race. They all seem stronger, thicker at the joints, straighter in the neck.

"Runners steady . . . *Go!*" My voice dissolves in the tailwind of runners.

At the mile, Dave and Tom are fighting off the top Perkiomen runner, and Sam George is battling the second. While Sam's body runs, his mind is outside of himself, surveying the scene like a general.

In the second mile, Dave slashes past his man while Tom drops back a few seconds. Sam and his nemesis, though, cling to each other through the second and third miles like two spent swimmers, each forcing the other to drown so that one might live.

Through the gate by the soccer field, their race erupts into a sprint. As he pulls his knees up and up, Sam's baritone breathing heaves. But the Perkiomen runner, short and stealthy, whisks past into the chute.

Just beyond the line, one second behind his toe, Sam falls to the ground. He writhes and moans, kicking at the grass with nightmarish throes.

But, in a minute, he is up, swinging his legs cheerfully, popping the top of a Gatorade.

After he looks over my shoulder at my clipboard, he lets loose a whoop. His time, 19:35, is by far his best, and symbolic, too—breaking through the twenty-minute threshold is immensely significant. Moreover, it speaks to continued improvement. He is ecstatic in the most literal sense of the word: out of his body. He is freed of the worry that his body cannot do what his mind wants it to do.

As Josh crosses the line, Sam counts on his fingers. The boys have clearly won. He lets out another whoop.

A minute later, Samantha climbs the shallow hill to the finish line, doggedly trying to collapse the two seconds between her and the Perkiomen girl.

But she runs out of time.

Nevertheless, her pace, 20:57, is her best for the season. She is unmoved by the time. Striding slowly away from the finish line, Samantha is thinking. In each of her eyes, I see a digit: two seconds. I wonder if she can see past them.

Sam and Samantha leave together with the shy distance and the subtle proximity of a couple.

Miraculously, there is room on this team for two Sams.

THE NEXT PRACTICE, to keep our spirits high for our race against Warren Hills two days from now, I decide it's time for another game. I wait for the team to assemble before I explain the rules. The older boys gather around me, penning me in with their size.

I, in turn, size them up. At their core, Sam George presides, wearing the same black socks he has worn in every practice and every race this season so far.

"Sam," I ask. "Just how many pairs of black socks do you have?"

He eyes his ankles fondly. "One."

"You wear the same socks every day?"

"These are the only ones that are comfortable."

"You gotta get some new socks," I exclaim, getting ready to insist, but because the team is around me, I can focus on Sam no more.

I divide the twenty-six runners into two groups and explain the game: each group will have a turn to chase and catch the other. The first team will disperse through campus; then, after three minutes, the second team will set out in pursuit. The members of the second must try to tag as many members of the first as they can within the space of twenty minutes. After the twenty minutes, the first team will do the same to the second.

I bolt off as part of the first team, anxious about pursuers, encouraging people to double up, to play strategically. Gretchen, Leyla, and I move like moles around the crowded field hockey field, barricading ourselves behind the pretty, ponytailed girls and their battering of sticks on balls.

We are swiftly routed from our hiding place by Sam George and a few of his henchmen, chased through a compost heap, and tagged by the pond. Other members of Sam's group scour the rest of campus, easily sweeping through the entirety of our ranks in just fourteen minutes.

It is Sam George's time to hide, and my team is pessimistic. Because we lose a lot of time cornering Samantha, twenty minutes pass without our catching Sam.

We wait for him to emerge and gloat. But the colors of the sky begin to burn and bleed. Slowly, the other runners wander off to meet rides and catch buses. Daylight smolders into night. The sky is an expanse of plum.

A dark shadow, coming from the field hockey field, limps toward me.

"Sit down," I say.

When I get Sam's sneakers and socks off, I am shocked. Sam's ankle is as dark as his socks, an improbable velvety richness. Streaks of purple ring his anklebone. The top of his foot is blue. The whole appendage is plumping up with greenish fluids. It is hot to the touch.

"Sam, you have to see a doctor."

He doesn't speak. He is afraid of doctors, casts, and time.

"It's going to take a little time to recover from that," I warn him.

"But my times will get slower."

I help Sam walk to his car. I talk about rest and recovery, but neither Sam—who he is or who he wants to be—is listening.

Sam thought he had all the time in the world to get the time he desired. But time is never what we expect. Though Sam's times have steadily improved, from race to race, from terrain to terrain, some Sam within him hooked his foot on a minute and fell over.

I walk into the school, hollow at the loss of another Sam, and there is Samantha, in the student lounge, still in her running clothes, conjugating Spanish verbs.

Thankfully, I have one Sam left.

Samantha's time has come, and with her time, the girls'. "Time," in that sense, is an appointed, fated moment, an apex, an archetype. As a result, only one Sam could be Sam, the winner. Samantha is able to accept that singularity, to weave together the parts within herself.

So I go into the school's office and call Warren Hills to make sure they have a full girls' team. Then I let Samantha know that they, in fact, do. Looking up from her Spanish verbs, she smiles like an angel with Pippi Longstocking hair.

A row of platform shoes lines the shower of the girls' locker room. Moravian Academy's field hockey goalie stores them there, "Just in case." The other girls, who are changing out of their school clothes for field hockey, tennis, and cross country, do not think to ask her, "Just in case *what*?" They all know a girl must look her best.

Katie and Kristy, whose feet are their livelihood, are not so excessive about their shoes. Katie's narrow sandals and Kristy's thicker hiking boots wait patiently in front of lockers as they change into running shoes for their race against Warren Hills today.

Water runs. Lockers slam. The colors of skin, so many shades of chalk, bark, and tea, shine like wax. Out of school clothes at last, Katie and Kristy pause to savor the moment between corduroys and red-and-white uniforms.

"He is *such* an idiot!" The field hockey goalie storms in, thunking her backpack to the floor. She stomps a well-heeled foot, her strong quadriceps tightening, defined by slim, nylon pants. Jewelry rattles. Fingernails glint.

The other girls on the field hockey team know immediately which boy she is talking about. They commiserate, sharing the names of other idiots, doing their best to convert the goalie's anger into amusement. They tell stories, incrementally exaggerating the depiction of idiocy. Finally, the goalie's marigold hair flutters as she bursts into laughter. In a moment of harmony that seldom happens in a high school, the rest of the girls in the locker room, from the glamorous field hockey players to the self-contained runners, join in.

Katie and Kristy laugh a little less long, then resume their dressing. They knew who the idiots were long ago.

Perfume muffles the sourness of cleats. Brushes sweep back curtains of hair. The stained tile floor is awash with cobalt silk, crimson velvet, and ash-colored stockings, still holding the shapes of legs.

Though our school's dress code prescribes a collared-shirt-and-tie uniform for boys, the specifications for girls are much muddier; they have more choices, more responsibility to fashion trends, more necessity to find clothes that make them attractive. During the class day, short girls wear long dresses, tall girls wear short skirts, and athletic girls wear form-fitting pants in glossy, synthetic fibers.

Those clothes, so carefully chosen in the morning, now drape the narrow wooden benches of the locker room; they twist in heaps on the floor; they spill from oversized gym bags like deflated dolls. The girls, quickly forgetting the boys, pull chiffon and baby-soft cotton over their heads and clap on baggy shorts and fleece. Gretchen and Leyla walk in, wearing black and lavender, new colors for the gardenlike floor.

"Who has socks I can borrow?" someone shouts. Balled-up athletic socks fly through the air.

"Who has a scrunchy?" Hair vanishes into tight ponytails.

"Who has a Band-Aid?" calls Leyla.

"I do," I say. I fish through my bag for my store of Band-Aids, athletic tape, and moleskin. I pull two strips out and place them on the bench in front of Leyla. Her bare feet, purplish from the cold floor, are spangled with rough old calluses and shiny new blisters.

The field hockey players scamper off en masse, hair swishing, playfully jostling each other with touches and words. Though the locker room has thinned, the cross country runners are lingering, ritualizing their actions to prepare for the race ahead of them. Over her uniform, Katie wears the basketball shirt her mother wore in high school, slate blue with navy rings tipping the collar and sleeves. Kristy, who has been carefully lacing her canvas ankle brace, pulls a thick sock over it.

When the girls emerge from the locker room with sticks or rackets or empty arms—like Kristy and Katie—they are dressed the same as the boys, who are surging from their own locker room. In a cyclone of motion on the gym floor, boys and girls blur together then fly from the building as one entity.

But clothing is a thin veil over a body. Kristy, the girls' captain, is small and muscular, a multisport athlete with a chronically bad ankle to prove it. Katie, a veteran runner of three years, is skinny as a flowerless stem. They both, though, constitute the depth of the girls' team, the essential fourth and fifth runners whose finishing places are as crucial to a winning score as the superhero who comes in first. Though a varsity team consists of the top seven runners, the race for a team victory is most often run in the muddy middle, the realm inhabited by Kristy and Katie.

Kristy and Katie wade together into the bright afternoon, slightly away from the bouquet of field hockey players moving toward the lower fields by the pond, the posse of handsome soccer players moving toward the upper fields above the pond, and even the boys on the cross country team. Both have bad ankles; both are conscious not to favor them. Each gives a sense that she is moving through shallow water, Kristy pushing through it, water splashing up against her thighs, Katie stepping high, dangling her toes above the water's surface. Both have their own ways of dealing with the race to come, with the pain it will aggravate in their ankles, their knees, their shoulders, with the doubt that will fracture their sense of themselves.

Though they know little about Warren Hills, a team from New Jersey, they are fully aware that this is the first pure race they have run: one-on-one against another team, no Liberty or late buses to confuse the situation.

When the Warren Hills school bus arrives, Kristy watches, counting the number of girls who file from the bus: seven, a full team. All seven are bigger than our runners, with substantial legs and defined arms. They wear their hair down, curled, teased, and wild.

Reaching back, Kristy touches the stubby brush of her hair.

Katie's tiny nose moves left, right.

But they keep looking, measuring.

As soon as the Warren Hills team walks the course, Kristy calls the girls into a circle.

"Yes, *Mother*," jokes Gretchen, trying out her new

nickname for Kristy. The other girls giggle approvingly. As Gretchen steps up to Kristy's shoulder, she is welcomed, with a hug, into the curve of Kristy's body. Their skin weaves together. The other girls cluster tightly around them. Their closeness to each other has the effect of holding hands. They are connected through arms, legs, entire bodies.

"We can win this," begins Kristy. Though she has rehearsed these words, her tone whirs and flutters with unexpected feeling. As the girls nod, ponytails sway. "Everyone has to run their best race." Faces are sober, but emotions throb, with blood, in a matrix of veins and nerve endings beneath the surfaces of skin. "Let's do it!" A thrill ripples from body to body so that even when Katie and the others move away, they are mysteriously tethered.

Under the sinewy tree by the starting line, Kristy, sole captain without Sam George running, leads stretches for both the boys and the girls. The air is caterpillar soft. Gems of light, half-hidden, twinkle around Kristy's feet. Usually the team's stretching, affected by the bulk of arms and legs, is helter-skelter, but today it is well choreographed. Appendages, somehow, are lighter; internal organs smaller; lids of eyes gone so that vision is unimpaired. Conscious of parents gathering around them, they are unafraid of being watched.

"Down to the left!" shouts Kristy. In unison, torsos fall. Fingers graze toes. Lips graze knees.

"Down to the right!" In unison, waists shift. Elbows brush thighs. Palms brush ankles.

Pivoting her body left and right against the backdrop of russet and moon-colored trees, turning the other runners like teacups, Kristy feels that they have no bad sides.

The sun blares like a trumpet above and just to the left of the starting line.

Kristy leads the girls to the line where they disperse, quiet in their tension, wholly in awe of the moment.

Boys file in between the girls, the top boys from both teams parallel to the top girls; the pattern follows with second and third. Mingled like that, the myriad of differences between boys and girls—the velvet and the smells—matters not at all.

"Runners steady . . . *Go!*" I shout.

And they do, light as flames.

The burden of winning, for each runner, is the weight of her body. That weight is the inverse of desire. When I see the girls, again, at the mile mark, I will know which has canceled the other out by the airiness or solidity of their footfalls.

Sam George, with the official stopwatch, limps alongside me to the mile mark. Shortly after Dave, Tom, and a pair of their rivals pass, the first two Warren Hills girls blitzkrieg through. The curls of their hair paint dark lines against the hollows of their cheeks.

Samantha is fifteen seconds behind them.

Sam and I, intent on our watches, don't speak to each other.

Twenty seconds behind Samantha, in a quiet pocket, Leyla scurries. Ten seconds later, Gretchen, Kristy, Holly, and Katie pass together in a diamond configuration. Their eyes forward, they seem unconscious of each other, but the cut-diamond shape does not alter. Their feet, though, do not hit the ground at the same time. Kristy and Katie's timing is by far the most disparate. For every step Katie takes with her seabird legs, Kristy's muscular calves shuffle through two and a third.

Katie should be moving faster.

Kristy should be moving slower.

But they stay together, connected by air, the moving core of the team.

At the two-mile mark, Samantha forty-five seconds behind the first two Warren Hills girls, I fear the race is lost, that this season will be like every season for the girls' team: warmth, personality, and laughter just veiling disappointment.

On my way to the finish line, I pass the field hockey practice: heads are lowered above sticks in the fierce waltz of their game. No bright eyes look up as Samantha, Leyla, Gretchen, Holly, Kristy, and Katie skirt the field, a quarter of a mile from the finish line of the race.

At the line, my fears about the race are confirmed.

The two Warren Hills girls beat Samantha by nearly a minute. Samantha walks off in search of water, thighs stiff, without a word.

But when Leyla, Gretchen, Kristy, Holly, and Katie cross the line, the numbers quickly, miraculously, add up. The girls have won, 26–29.

A long chain of hugs passes from body to body, reaching out to Samantha and drawing her deep into the clutch of girls.

Some might say that depth is mind, some soul. But I say depth is the place in the body where pain resides, because that is the place with no bottom. If you can accept that pain without being swallowed up by it, then you have depth.

You run with your legs and arms; you run with your heart. But you win with your entire self.

ON MONDAY, autumn kisses deeply. The wind is whistling so high it seems to be signaling a message of either distress or hope. On our warm-up run, some bodies cut through the wind, but Kristy's meets it straight. It pushes her back; she pushes it back. It is a large war fought in a small space.

As we run past the practice fields, the field hockey players are lined up, hitting toward the goal. The goalie, a cage over her face, is smacking away the volley of balls with every part of her body. Her marigold hair licks from the back of her headgear, sweat turning the ends of it to blackened points. She is wonderful to watch.

By the end of the half-mile run to the lacrosse field, Kristy is winded. Nevertheless, she doesn't forget she is captain. She tightens her arms, lifts her hands over her head, and calls out instructions, her body and her words perfect mirrors for each other.

Halfway through our stretches, Katie joins us. She drops to the ground, butterflies her legs, and presses her feet to the ground. The cartilage in her knees under the taut skin appears to be smiling with bright molars. Though she is holding on to her ankles, apparent over her socks is a line of athletic tape that signals she has, officially, joined the ranks of the injured.

She is intent on her stretching. Lunging one knee forward, she balances herself on stamen wrists to stretch the calf of her straight leg. In a pistonlike motion, she shifts knees efficiently and stretches the calf of the other leg. The muscle swells like a pearl on the lip of a polished shell.

With everyone else, Katie rises, stretching complete, her ankle feverish, her lower leg raspberry-colored and sore, but her head empty of doubt.

Her butternut hair grazes the nibs of her shoulder blades.

We walk to the bottom of a small hill along the country road that runs past campus. There, over the wind, I explain the workout: we will alternately skip, bound, and run to the top of the hill, then jog back down, three times for each exercise. I illustrate the bounding motion, the form that is used in the triple jump. It is a tricky maneuver that strains the hamstrings and the lower back.

I watch Katie practice the motion, leaping along the side of the road, and I am startled by how small the small of her back is.

As we line up in pairs at the bottom of the hill, Kristy pulls me aside. "This is really going to hurt my ankle," she says.

"Stop if it hurts," I insist, holding my hands up as if to save her from jumping off a precipice. I'm serious: losing another runner, at this point, would be like losing my own leg.

But when she bounds up the hill for the first time, side by side with Katie, she pulls on her arms so aggressively, as if they can lift the lower part of her anatomy with ropes, that her feet just graze the pavement. At the top of the hill, slowing to make the U-turn to the descent, her shoulders tremble slightly. Her face, though, registers no pain.

Katie, in contrast, is using the small of her back, a hinge for her thighs, to pull herself upward so that her feet do not smack the ground. At the top of the hill, she bends her spine this way and that, but she still looks backward and laughs at the antics of the freshman boys.

"How do you feel?" I ask them as the three of us jog side by side down the hill.

"It hurts," Kristy says simply, conversationally.

Katie only signals her agreement; she is focusing on her form, on its origins at the small of her back, on its conclusion at the tips of her toes.

Together, they fall into line behind Gretchen and Leyla, this time to skip up the hill. They laugh with the other girls as their arms and back lift them higher and higher with each skip.

The body is a utopia; the strength of a limb or an organ or a sense compensates for the weakness of another. Kristy's arms and the small of Katie's back, today, are all altruism. Because of them, they will sleep well tonight out of guilt-free exhaustion, peace.

They continue to skip, to bound, to run until, by the end, they are not alone in their pain. Everyone's hurting equally. Oliver's mouth is crooked. Tom is muttering about lunch, hand on his stomach. Dave is holding his knee up with one hand, kneading the base of his hamstring.

Still as cornstalks, Katie and Kristy let their gazes climb the hill once more. I suspect they knew that—despite their injuries—their pain in the end would not surpass the pain of the others. Nor would it surpass the pain they would feel if they were completely healthy, strong as goddesses, league and district champions. Their desire for these things, no matter how great, should eclipse the burden of their bodies, but it can never make the pain go away.

Just as we are never to look directly at a solar eclipse, we are never, as spectators, able to watch races in their entirety. But, catching another glimpse of Katie as she fiddles with the tape that circles her ankle, I see her torso bending over her foot, springing from the locus in the small of her back. Remarkable. I think of the field hockey players hunched over their sticks and ponder: How can they help but watch the brief but bright crescents of a race that they are offered?

The small of the back, the place we can't see, is a connecting point between the upper and lower body. We are full of such points, intersections of bone, blood, and energy. Most of them are smaller than the small of the back, but they are neither more nor less fragile. That our bodies hold together at all, with the pressures we put on them, is a miracle.

Bodies are miraculous. Like bodies of water, they flood, recede, but do not lose their integrity.

THE NEXT DAY, everyone is hurting, straggling behind their friends on their way to classes, struggling with forks at lunch, lingering too long in the locker rooms. Katie and Kristy vanish to the trainer. After an abbreviated warm-up, we run a moderate distance at a moderate pace around the campus. The fall air is minty. Its cleanliness tickles. After a few laps, everyone is happy to stop, stand still, and breathe.

Because no one is in any hurry to move, my assistant coach, Tom Schoeninger, suggests that it's time to establish personal goals. We are at the halfway point in the season, the cusp of September and October. Time, the leaves just beginning to fall fragrantly, and the tension between sleepiness and strength in bodies all welcome such musings.

Tom presses the clipboard to his broad chest and pulls a ballpoint pen from the pocket of his blue tennis shorts. We point fingers at Dave and Samantha, predicting home-course records for them. For others, we look at their time in the Warren Hills race and subtract a minute or so, more for some than others. The exercise is fun, a game of chance. Gretchen and Leyla nudge me to dream for them, to prophesy speed that will become real in the writing of it: so official in black ink on the spreadsheet.

Kristy, though, snubs numbers. "My goal," she informs me, Gretchen and Leyla listening, too, "is for the girls' team to be league champions."

There is no space in the rigid grid of the spreadsheet for that statement. Personal goals are tightly contained . . . individual. They encompass everything over which one has direct control. That way, the *person* can fulfill them. Tom's pen hovers.

Kristy, though, is waiting for us to register her goal officially, to post it publicly, to acknowledge it as a viable reality. She doesn't think she's asking too much.

As the fall dusk breathes eucalyptus and parsley smells over our bare arms and legs, I shiver.

Hearing what Kristy said, Katie and Holly join Gretchen and Leyla. They nod at Kristy then look up, waiting for the pen to move.

"You can win leagues," I say. "You can do well at districts."

Tom chimes in, "But as for your personal goal, Kristy . . ." He jots a number down: 22:30, over a minute faster than her time against Warren Hills.

She glances at the grid and shrugs. The pen, to her, is no prophet. She has, on her own, defined her goal.

BETWEEN CLASSES the next day, I see Katie in the hallway. She is sporting a new haircut: sharp, butternut lines arc around her doll-like face. With the hair, a dark blue pea coat, and flared pants, she looks like something out of *The Avengers*. Pale lavender veins pulse beneath the talcum skin of her neck.

"Ms. Pont, yesterday you started the warm-up run without me again."

I wince, remembering she went to see the trainer. "I know. I won't do it today."

I skulk into the rest of my day.

School over, the team gathers noisily in the back parking lot. The day is moist, bluish in hue. Legs emerging stickily from shorts have lost their summer sun. Shins are ivory; the scars on knees are cold as quartz. But blood is warm. Rested from the easy workout yesterday, boys and girls race across the macadam in games of cat and mouse. It takes all my energy to gather them together and load them into vehicles.

For practice, we're driving to the path along the Lehigh River for another out-and-back. Now, at the edge of September, we'll run five minutes farther upriver than the last time we were there; we'll return at a significantly faster pace. We're ready: as the body gets stronger, the workouts get harder. We'll feel it, but in a new way. At a certain point, muscle and joint are no longer pain's domain, so it arcs, kamikaze-like, for the body's depths . . . for bone, for marrow. Landing, it grows in a glacial development that makes itself known late at night, doing homework, or worse, in sleep, jerking Katie and Kristy awake so they are tired all the next day. That tiredness, though, is satisfying: it is the result of desire, of strength, of pushing the body further than it knows it can go, and of saying to pain, churlishly, "I'm watching you."

I am a mile away from school, my car full of yammering. Kristy's voice, panicked, suddenly rises above the others: "Where's Katie?"

"Aagh!" I imagine Katie's butternut hair, her tiny nose, her mouth moving as she chastises me.

I make a U-turn and look in my rearview mirror after.

I drive through campus to the building in which the trainer's room is located. As I am about to jump out, Oliver cries, "There she is!" Katie is walking up the path to the classroom buildings. I wonder which is the quickest way to follow the driveway around: left or right. As I am thinking, Katie vanishes beneath the shadow of a tree.

I accelerate, driving straight up the narrow walkway toward her. A cheer rises from the back of the car. When I pull up beside Katie, she is all smiles. As she opens the door to the backseat, she laughs, incredulous, not at all aware of how important she is.

"I was in the training room forty-five minutes," she explains.

"What takes so long in there?" I ask.

"Those soccer goons," she says. "They need every part of their body taped."

As she offers details, we all laugh at the idiocy she describes.

The rest of the team is waiting by the river for us, looking forward to what has become their favorite run.

Along the river, more blue sky appears between the forking branches. The river seems closer, the ground browner, bodies more familiar with those running nearby. Everyone, as planned, runs farther, faster. Though I only singled out the top five, all seven varsity girls run the full twenty-five minutes out. They make the decision personally, and, following Kristy's lead, they know it's the right choice.

At the end of the run, everyone's breathing is hard, sucking the vitality out of the afternoon. In under a minute, though, the need to breathe seems miraculously inconsequential.

The girls look upriver. They could do it again, farther, faster.

As we walk back to the cars, my thigh is throbbing. I know I pulled a muscle two days before when we bounded up the hills. I can hardly think to drive. An injury, no matter how minuscule, saps strength from the rest of the body. I snap at Oliver to stop fiddling with the radio dial.

When we return to school, I limp to the training room myself, kneading the pain in my quadriceps with my palm.

The other sports' practices have just ended. A line of boys six deep—some with buzz cuts, some tattoos, some tie-dye—is getting ankles, shoulders, and thighs attended to, while field hockey players dig their manicured fingers into an enormous jar of candy. This is the world that Katie cannot penetrate. I, too, hang shyly back while these, the cool boys and girls, flirt full force.

I wait forty-five minutes before it's my turn to hop up on the padded table.

Taking my foot into his hands, the trainer stretches my leg out. "Does that hurt?"

"No"

"That?"

"No."

"That?"

"Yes."

"You shouldn't run for a couple of days." He releases my leg.

I jump up, trying to measure, for myself, the depth of my pain.

Judging when to stop, rest, and recover or when to run through an injury is—for most little aches and pains—impossible. The decision stems from the individual's denial, endurance, or compensating strengths.

I knew already what the trainer would say. On the drive back to school, feeling weak, I wanted the rest, the recovery, the release from pain. But now, looking around the training room, I'm thinking: not a chance. If Kristy and Katie can run through pain, so can I.

They are my compensating strength. No, I should say—as Kristy would—we are all compensating strengths for one another. That's how we mesh as a team.

———

FOR A WEEK, training for our next race, Katie's tape peels on and off; Kristy's ankle swells and recedes within the embrace of her laces.

ON A SOUPY, Indian summer day, early October, the boys and girls are divided. The boys have a race at Belmont Plateau in Philadelphia against several all-male teams from our league. The girls remain home to run Pius, which doesn't have a full girls' team, and, more importantly, Pen Argyl, which is a public school reported to be good competition.

I opt to drive the seven members of the boys' varsity on the long, tricky route to Philadelphia while my assistant, Tom, will stay with the girls and also the boys' junior varsity, who are a good match for Pius.

It's the practical thing to do, I assure myself.

"You know what to do," I say to Kristy.

"Of course," she smiles. Clearly, she likes the idea that the girls will have the race to themselves.

As I am contemplating what snacks and tunes to bring in the van for the hour-long drive, where we will eat afterward, and how well the boys will do in the race itself, Kristy is making her own plans.

"We're going to win," she tells the other girls. "Pen Argyl can't be that good."

Carrying a case of Gatorade cans to the van, I run into Mrs. Worsley.

"Setting up for the race?" she asks me.

"Actually I'm taking this to Philadelphia. The boys are running there, and I'm driving them."

"Sexist," she says.

"I know the way to Philadelphia," I rationalize. "Besides, Tom's from Pen Argyl. He knows the coach. He knows their girls."

"I'm kidding!" teases Mrs. Worsley.

But I hate having to make the choice. Though I know coaching during a race is irrelevant, I want the pleasure of watching the girls. If they beat Pen Argyl, as they should, I will not witness their joy, beading on their skin like sweat, coursing from their arms in hugs, transforming their voices into music.

As I am driving, I feel the heat in my lungs and imagine other lungs, back home: Leyla's hummingbird breaths, nervous on her warm-up run. My foot cramps up from the gas pedal, and I imagine other feet: Kristy's ankle, safe in its brace. The small of my back chafes against the vinyl seat; I imagine the small of Katie's back, so much stronger than it looks.

As I walk the grass-and-gravel course that the boys will run, I see Katie's ankle, turning then straightening, without a moment's hesitation. As the boys stretch, I watch Kristy growing until she becomes a dome, sheltering Katie, Gretchen, Leyla, and the rest.

As the gun sounds at Belmont Plateau and forty-seven

boys spread out along a grassy hill, I hear the single, simultaneous heartbeat of the girls' team as they begin their own race.

Empathy is a painful thing, regardless of the person with whom you are empathizing. It forces you to be yourself and someone else, to shoulder a second body, a second mind.

Whatever is going on at home, it is joyous, painful, real.

Dave wins the race; the boys' team soundly beats four of the five other schools and is just a few points away from winning. But I am devoured by my desire to match my feelings for the race back home to the facts about it.

Did the girls win?

Outside a restaurant in downtown Philadelphia, with the school's cellular phone, we call a junior varsity boy, the only phone number we know. Samantha won the race, he reports.

The boys cheer.

"What about the team?" I urge.

He doesn't know.

I turn off the phone, dismayed. No one knows how to watch a race, not even other runners. No one watched the miraculous counterpoint of Katie and Kristy's strides, the juxtaposition that caused the team to win against Warren Hills and might have done so again today against Pen Argyl.

The entire drive home, the small of my back itches with impatience.

In my mailbox at school, Tom left me the stats from the race.

The girls lost to Pen Argyl, 32–23.

Looking at the stats, I notice how close to each other our third, fourth, and fifth girls finished, just behind a runner from Pen Argyl. Too close, I think. They should have run their own races, sought out their own goals: staying together slowed them down. I picture it, see that one or two might have passed the Pen Argyl girl, might have sought out and breezed by others. I am angry at them, angry at myself for not being there, angry that their regular-season record—discounting invitationals—is 1–1, numbers so muddy they say nothing.

The Moravian Academy girls' cross country team has never had a winning season, and I want it as badly as they do.

So I force myself to look at the stats again. A new idea emerges, not written in numbers, but suggested by the proximity of names, of bodies. They were, in that muddy center of the race, tethered together, body to body, just as they were when they beat Warren Hills.

If they win, or if they lose, they do it together.

I think of Kristy's personal goal. It has become the goal of all those girls, I see, and each win or loss now is a preparation to meet the final, the real, goal.

I correct myself. Staying together made them fast.

Staying together in that race, they were a team—and they will continue to be through the rest of our races against other schools, through the district race, through the league race.

Staying together, they are depth.

6. Gravity's Rainbow

*D*ave doesn't like to run alone.

With Sam Cohen and Sam George still injured, the possibilities for running partners are narrow. To provide companions, I call optional practices on weekends. Dave and I meet on Saturday mornings, leaning on the backs of cars with Leyla, Tom, and a few other souls who shiver in the morning dampness until, deciding no one else will show, we run along the narrow roads that flank the campus. Depending on the pace,

Dave has the company of all or one, with whom he chats, his salmon gums visible as he smiles and breathes.

Today, late September, he describes his algebra class while curry-colored leaves, still moist with life, skim past our shoulders.

"We keep journal entries," he tells Tom, who is acing calculus but is side by side with Dave in the advanced physics class.

"What do you write?" Tom asks, incredulous.

"We write about how we feel about math." As he runs, collarbone and chin folded inward, he describes construction-paper cutouts of geometric shapes that the teacher passes around the room. "We write about how we feel about rectangles."

"Why are you in that class?" I ask.

"I never learned my times tables."

But distance multiplies easily despite morning fog, sluggishness, and grumbling stomachs; Dave moves rapidly, naturally, Tom and I working like machines to keep up. The two boys are slightly apart from each other, slightly away from the edge of the road, free from friction or the gravitational pull of minor bodies. Neither of them has pretty form: Dave is knotted, Tom cumbersome. But the torque of their strides, with each revolution of the legs, allows them to reach a line, visible only to them, that they touch simultaneously.

Then, with instantaneous measurement, they find the next line.

Dave, looking up, seeing, then forgetting all else, reaches a hand out to catch a falling leaf. On this team, we all believe that catching a leaf brings luck. There is no art to it; the leaf either lands in your hand or doesn't come close. He waves his arm back and forth to follow the leaf's dizzying motion, follows it to the center of the street, but it, at the last instant, twists away from his fingers. Disappointed, Dave stutter-steps to catch himself and again finds his place beside Tom, who has not missed a stride. Tom is glad to, once again, share the pace.

I wonder if Tom or anyone else can replace Sam George, Dave's best friend, and I wonder, too, if Sam's injury is that which punctures Dave with the teeth of solitude, bleeding him, a little bit, of the desire to run.

Next Saturday, Dave and I alone pry open the bivalve of sleep. Though it is only a few hundred yards from where I live, I drive up to the school just seconds before our meeting time. There, Dave waits by himself on the bumper of his truck, arms crossed, legs braided.

Today, he is wearing a yellow thrift-store windbreaker, puckered around the zipper, that matches the crusty yellow paint of his pickup truck. Though he is thin and blinkingly frail, his face, limbs, and extremities are roughened and burned. The veins on the back of his hands are plump beneath oat-colored skin from work on his family's farm; the vein in the center of his forehead plumps from thought about everything else.

Three days before the race at Belmont Plateau, we squint with precoffee eyes in the mottled morning, each of us secretly angry at the other for creating this moment, each of us secretly relieved that someone created the moment for us. Neither could do it alone.

I have other secrets: I secretly think Dave will win Tuesday's race against five other league teams at Belmont Plateau, will break our course record before the end of the season, will do well enough in districts to make states, could win our league. With both Sams injured, my secret hopes for Dave constrict my heart. I want more from him, I suspect, than he wants from himself. That fear is my greatest secret, and it makes me feel the most lonely.

Though Dave in our race against Perkiomen ten days ago surpassed Tom as the lead runner on the boys' team, took the number one place overall for the first time in his career, and has steadily improved through every race and practice, he keeps what he thinks or desires a secret. He watches the joints of his fingers as he bends them in the sunlight.

"Did you have coffee?" I ask wistfully.

He shakes his head, and we gaze at each other empathically, lonely and longing for coffee.

But we rub our groaning eyes and see the day is dry and clean as flour.

"We should do some hills," I say, more cheerfully.

"All right," he says. "Where?"

"Hackett's?" It's the first place that comes to mind, but not a first choice. Hackett's Park is, even in the forgiving selectivity of memory, immeasurably grueling.

"Sure."

My heart clutches, but I keep my fear of the hill a secret.

We climb into my car, and I fiddle with knobs for music and heat to avoid thinking about the hills we are about to face.

As another tactic, I coach as I drive. "You need to run your first mile faster. You should be close to five minutes."

He shakes his head. "I don't think like that."

"How do you think?"

"I just try to run a little faster than I think I can and hope for the best."

"So that's your secret?"

He shrugs, revealing nothing.

I decide to expose my secret. "You know"—I turn the car's heat down—"you really could beat the course record by the end of the season."

But he doesn't respond.

"You could make it to states," I venture.

Still, he doesn't respond.

"After the race in Philadelphia, we'll get cheese steaks," I bribe.

Again, no response.

"How far are you into *Gravity's Rainbow*?"

And he happily chronicles each banana image in the novel through page 150.

"I never made it past page one hundred," I say.

The book is a little like the hills in Hackett's Park. The place is a strange array of inclines and plateaus that culminates in a parking lot, a set of picnic tables, a rusty faucet, and an old cannon. For a practice, we use a dizzyingly steep, grassy slope and a long, curving driveway, known as the "Cannon," each of which concludes at the picnic tables. We sprint three of each, alternating back and forth, in between walking a bit then jogging around a softball field on a midlevel plateau till we are ready to stride up another hill.

"What order do you want to do them in?" I ask Dave as we shed our jackets, thinking he will choose something creative. He stretches, lifting his arms so that the blue, red, and yellow Superman decal on his T-shirt crackles.

He opts to tackle the grassy slope first: standard procedure. After jogging around the softball field twice, we cut through the chain-link fence, swoop down the yellowing field, dodge the gaping doorways of groundhogs, and veer sharply left at the tree line, side by side, our strides reaching for the same invisible line.

But he has found another line, one I can't see: he is halfway up the hill in an instant.

While I am fighting the stubborn center of the hill, he vanishes over the rise at the top.

On the far side of the parking lot, by the picnic tables, he is bent over his knees, gasping. He looks back at me, mouth slightly parted. He had forgotten, I can see, that I exist.

Somewhere on that hill, he found the way to be alone.

Together, we begin the ritual walk to the softball field. "If I beat you on the Cannon," I say as we begin jogging, "you owe me a lollipop."

I feel more confident with a goal. Though in the past two years I have beaten him on the longer, gradual hill consistently, I know he's now stronger than he was as a sophomore or junior and should beat me. But we'll be close, within reaching distance of each other most of the way up the hill. Because of our proximity, we will sense each other's secret thoughts—anger, relief, and the other private feelings that undermine and fuel a run of any magnitude or altitude.

At the base of the hill, by a yellow metal sign that I slap to signal the start, we sprint, side by side, toward the first bend in the driveway.

At the second bend, he loses me.

At the top, he finds himself alone again. As I pant up behind him, he looks at me as if my presence is a surprise, as if he had not thought about me or anyone else for a very long time.

Four more times we begin close and end as far away as humans can be.

Trying to stifle my syrupy gasps, I regard his gentle sweat, his slightly apologetic demeanor. I want to shake him out of the inexplicable, almost naive talent he possesses. I want him to be angry and greedy with desire.

But all I can do is open up the back of my car for him. We sit on the tailgate, the bright morning light as solid as air can be, eating doughnuts and drinking juice. His long fingers splayed, he lifts the carton to his lips. His ankles crossed, his dark shins tighten and shine. His forearms, salted with sweat, glow like mussel shells. He tells me about insects, radio evangelists, Haruki Murakami, and how many bales of hay he will load that day.

All the while, I sense, he is talking about running. But I cannot measure his metaphors.

Dave is a poet. And poets like Dave are the keepers of secrets; they swiftly perambulate the meaning of things, counting the pulse by avoiding the heart. Because I am too caught up in heart, beating me on some hills is easy for him. But he will not reveal what the beating means: if he runs to win or if he runs simply because running is something Sam George once wooed him to do.

Though good poets, like celestial bodies, pull and repel simultaneously, even they find it hard to be alone. In order to be so, they must forget friends. In that respect, Dave and Sam are equally tested, though their experiences have diverged and will continue to do so along the separate running trails that friends too often take.

THE TRIP TO BELMONT PLATEAU on October 7 is the first time the team has traveled without Sam George. I wonder how Dave feels to be alone now, facing a race that is notoriously difficult, a course on which time warps so that runners are a minute slower than usual. As I load the school's van with Gatorade and foil-wrapped baked goods, I remember a story Sam George told me: in fifth grade, when he was first visiting Moravian Academy he saw Dave, a skinny, spectacled boy, slowly perambulating the playground. Sam promptly picked Dave up and deposited him in a Dumpster.

Sam says that touch connected Dave, for the first time, with space and time.

As we drive down the Pennsylvania Turnpike, we play car games, trivia tests that focus on letters and words. Dave is not excelling; in fact, he removes himself from the game in a snail-like manner, drawing himself slowly into the conchlike confines of his mind.

Game ended, we are listening to boy-music: Metallica, Pink Floyd, and Stevie Ray Vaughan. In the rearview mirror, I see Dave, his mouth, nostrils, and ears open to the world, but his eyes quite closed in sleep.

Black flies, wakened by the Indian summer heat,

buzz, confused, around weeds and trash barrels in Belmont Plateau's parking lot. We swat at them, squinty-eyed, as we hunt down bathrooms.

Walking the course, up the first hill, around the perimeter of the park, then into the woods along a dusty path, Bryan mimics a blues-guitar riff and Oliver ad-libs, "I got the cross country blues; I don't know what to do." Dave warms to the tune. Together, we look at trouble spots on the course: hairpin turns and grottos inhabited by Philadelphia's homeless.

After they have stretched, the boys sneak back to the van for Gatorade though I have warned them against drinking too much. They sit on the curb, swiping bees from the mouths of their cans. The strong sunlight darkens them: cool shadows stretch from their brows to the tops of their feet. When I approach, they push their crushed cans away and smile with complicitous innocence. They smirk at each other, thinking they have one-upped me.

I pick up the cans and deposit them in a barrel.

I could never be angry at a crime committed in the name of comfort or camaraderie. Dave, crowded between Bryan and Oliver, sitting on the low curb so that his long, driftwood shins bob before his face like Popsicle sticks, seems ready for recess, for kickball and capture the flag and Red Rover. As I shoo the boys to the starting line, I secretly hope this means Dave will win.

In order to do so, he must find himself alone in front

of the forty-six other runners who double up on the crooked, chalk-marked starting line.

For the first mile of the race, Dave is not alone. He is ten seconds behind the lead runner, from Sleighton, but he holds on to him with the hook of his eyes. Tom and Bryan, not far behind, are playing catch with a pair of Girard runners.

When the Sleighton runner and Dave vanish into the woods, the other forty-five runners filing after, I feel alone and frightened. Time, for me, warps; enough time elapses while I wait, it seems, for Dave to lose the race.

Suddenly emerging from the woods again, Dave is still not alone. He and the Sleighton runner, though, have switched places. Dave is out front. The second-place boy is within breathing distance, tall and muscular in a dark uniform. If he reaches out his arms, he could swallow Dave whole. Dave feels his presence because of the absence; he knows that he will see the other runner only when he passes him.

So Dave's body, moving forward, is also a barrier to what lies behind.

Dave's nostrils and eyes are onyx, his lips, elongated and flattened, are umber; his nose and jaw are sharp as arrowheads; his body is wire and terra-cotta. But he seems to run weightless, far above the ground. He loses the burden of the body behind him and the burden of the need for anybody else.

He wins by one second. Because of that second, he is all alone, the only way the winner can be.

Even as he walks, regaining his breath, he continues to float. It takes him a while to come down to us. All the other boys jostle around the clipboard, dripping silver sweat on the sizzling ground as I tally the score.

He becomes conscious of the noise and excitement in the van, everyone buzzing not only because we beat four of the other five teams in the race and lost to Girard due only to the absence of the Sams, but also because we are on our way to South Street for cheese steaks.

"We're *really* going to get cheese steaks?" Dave asks.

"I told you we would," I say.

But he still appears doubtful.

On South Street, tattooed men buy Beanie Babies and forty-ounce beers; women wobble on platform shoes; kids ride BMX bikes up and down the curbs. Though the boys have changed from their uniforms to casual clothes, they feel the sweat of the race close to them, solidifying. Dave's thrift-store shirt sticks to his chest. He is relieved to enter the air conditioning of a metallic diner.

Cheese steaks and french fries arrive in plastic baskets along with a rainbow of condiments contained in milky plastic. The waitress refills our Cokes several times. Tom finishes quickly and scavenges baskets for stray chips and pickles.

Outside, after I use the school's cellular phone to learn the outcome of the girls' race, Dave repeats, "I really didn't think we were actually going to get cheese steaks."

"We needed to celebrate," I say, though the excuse skirts the truth. Really, I just thought we would be like kids at playtime, happy in each other's company.

But I wonder about poets. Because they believe that language is inaccurate, they think the rest of us are liars.

So, when I tell Dave that he could win at Belmont Plateau, could break our course record, could do well enough in districts to make states, could win our league, he thinks I'm talking about literature or religion or some other truth.

He doesn't need to understand me to win, though, just as he doesn't need to know his multiplication tables to be an outstanding student in physics. Dave skips certain fundamental steps on his way to becoming who he is. As a result, I cannot calculate his future, cannot predict if he will win again.

The enigma of Dave is as maddening as a Pynchon novel.

NIMISH AND RAJEEV run together.

While Dave makes his way alone in Philadelphia, back at school Nimish runs with Rajeev on the junior varsity team against Pius and Pen Argyl, together like drumsticks, like candlesticks, like clapping hands, like holding hands, fine on their own, but more emphatic with the other.

Both slim and brown with large hands and feet, both lost in clothes, both peering critically over their glasses with eyes so dark they appear to be pupilless, they are hard to tell apart. That is their first and greatest joke, one that never grows old.

They have been friends since they were three. While she and her son were visiting with Rajeev's family, Nimish's mother cut short their stay, saying that Nimish needed a haircut. Upon hearing this, Rajeev took Nimish aside, brandished a pair of scissors, and snipped off Nimish's hair.

"Can he stay now?" Rajeev begged.

Nimish has, since, never left him.

I stand in the chamois light of the faculty room at Moravian Academy while Dave's truck and the cars of the other boys who ran at Belmont Plateau rumble and groan up the driveway. In my hand are the results of Nimish and Rajeev's race against Pen Argyl and Pius. The white sheets, blue-veined with grids, crackle like leaves in my hand. Using the numbers as the heart of the story, I build the imagery around it, can see Rajeev and Nimish running on the periphery of campus to warm up, whispering to each other the way birds do at dusk, high but private. The sunshine glitters and the shade is deep as caves.

Nimish and Rajeev tremble on the starting line, each turned slightly toward the other, their shoulders so narrow they inhabit the space of a single body.

For the first 800 meters, they run side by side. Nimish's shorter legs turn over quickly; Rajeev's legs, long and light, step high. The glasses, on both, magnify the surprise of their charcoal eyes.

Then Nimish takes a step forward, not because he wants to, but because his feet are lifting him in a way he cannot fight.

They run the last two and a half miles of the race progressively distant—five, ten, twenty, forty seconds apart—each imagining where the other is. When Nimish is on the road, hipbone skimming the guardrail, he sees Rajeev at the softball backstop; when Rajeev is in front of the headmaster's house, jawline tight as he hears his two-mile time, he knows Nimish is entering the gates of the school.

When Nimish finishes, at 21:59, he floats above the race, watching but not seeing, until Rajeev crosses the line, fifty-five seconds later.

They fall together like pages of a book. Their feet touch. Nimish points at Rajeev and laughs.

Rajeev makes a sour face. "You're just lucky," he says.

"Maybe I'm just faster," says Nimish.

"So what. I'm better than you at everything else," retorts Rajeev.

"Like what?" Nimish is incredulous.

Rajeev responds with a litany as they walk, tight to each other's side, toward the jug of Gatorade. The sounds of their bickering diminish to a buglike hum.

Though Nimish is the first Moravian runner against Pen Argyl and Pius, only twenty-nine seconds behind the top two finishers, both on the Pen Argyl varsity, and instrumental in the defeat of Pius and Pen Argyl, those statistics are mere facts. The race, as far as he is concerned, truly measured the ebb and flow of his friendship with Rajeev. They compete, but only to poke fun at the competition.

I hold the statistics in my hands, white paper marked with last names, first initials, and columns of numbers. The grid chronicles space and time. But the story, yet unwritten, tells of the gravitational pull and the slow release of friendship.

THE NEXT DAY THE TEAM, thirty or so waving branches, are gathered in the parking lot. Half-hidden, like colored eggs or mischief, Rajeev and Nimish play with sticks. It is an old shtick, and they are egged on by Oliver and Dave. They fight each other, smacking sticks, dancing around in mock fervor. Though the sticks touch, their bodies remain equidistant.

Seeing me, Rajeev loses his weapon and falls away from Nimish.

"Ms. Pont, can we play fox and hound?" He cocks his apple-shaped head to the side, his eyes like cloves behind his wired glasses.

I roll my own eyes. Tomorrow we are racing against Solebury at home; the day before competition is not the time for a game.

"*Please,* Ms. Pont?" He plumps his amber lips in a pout. The others are listening, wondering how I can resist his pull. I can't; he is so much smaller than me that I imagine his request can do no harm.

"All right," I concede. Solebury, I rationalize, won't give us much of a race.

Nevertheless, I let myself get caught early, doing my best to speed the game along. On the periphery of the field hockey field, I nab Nimish who works with me to track down Bryan.

The game concludes in half an hour; we do not bother with a cool-down run.

"Rest," I insist as the team wanders away, paths crooked, as if from a recess in which everyone fell on the blacktop and skinned a knee.

The next day, they appear rested, loose. The air is cool, pleasant. The Solebury team is slow to step up to the starting line, and we quickly snicker, smug in knowing how much like a game this victory will be.

Without competition, Dave and Tom push each other through the first mile. Then Dave, for the rest of the race, is alone. Tom, Bryan, Oliver, and Nimish, fighting off only two real competitors, secure the spots behind him.

Dave wins easily, so easily that his time, 17:59, is only seven seconds faster than that of his previous home race.

"You broke eighteen!" I exclaim.

Dave's expression is flat with dissatisfaction. "We shouldn't have played a game yesterday," he retorts.

"Dave, you won," says Sam George, standing nearby.

Dave responds with explanations as they walk, tight to each other's side, toward the jug of Gatorade. The sound of Dave's voice does not diminish in my mind. I have never before understood him so keenly. He has entered the world of competition, frustration, numbers, a world in which second place, exhaustion, and injury are communicable diseases.

Dave has learned to do without Sam.

Nimish, though, ran a race that far surpassed expectations. The fifth-place finisher for Moravian, Nimish has earned a spot on the varsity for the first time. With a time of 21:02, he is only two seconds away from his season's goal, and two minutes seven seconds in front of Rajeev.

Rajeev's game, it seems, was designed to help Nimish. Nimish cannot do without Rajeev.

Like a pair of gnats, the two of them scurry off, circling each other as they move swiftly forward. As they do, they grow smaller and smaller in the crimson October dusk until they become a single point.

ON SATURDAY, Dave arrives early, and Nimish follows, dropped off by his mother, who, from the murky interior of her minivan, smiles at me with a look full of motherly pride. When Leyla and Kristy join us, we load my car for Louise Moore Park.

As Dave paraphrases the plot of a movie, we circle the park. The day is gray, sullen. The bright days of fall, I sense, have passed. Time has delivered us to the slate days of late autumn, only two dual races left before the countdown to the district race.

Dave is as fast as he should be.

Nimish is not far behind.

While Dave and I wait for Nimish, our workout complete, we look over at a cluster of tables near the parking lot. They are empty, but we remember:

Once, not long ago, at one of those tables, small and cement with a checkerboard burned into the surface, Rajeev and Nimish sat facing each other. Between them, on the board, was nothing but space. Nevertheless, they deliberated. Rajeev's chin rested in his hand. Nimish's thoughts remained hidden behind glasses.

With contemplative exactness, Nimish moved a missing piece.

Rajeev responded in kind.

Now, alone, Nimish finishes his run. When Kristy

and Gretchen join us, we return to school. In the parking lot, I talk with Kristy as Gretchen climbs into her mother's car and Dave pulls away.

When Kristy leaves, I see Nimish pulling at the doors to the front of the school. They do not give. So he begins to run, at a cautious, long-distance pace, along the long wing of the building. His feet seem far too big for his legs, but he moves elegantly. When the wall ends, he cuts through the grass to the driveway and vanishes behind a chain-link fence.

"What the . . . ," I mutter. Then I realize: Nimish is running home by himself.

I jump into my car.

A mile up the road, I pull up beside him. He jogs in place, patiently waiting for me to state my business and drive away so that he can continue onward. His knees are twice the size of his calf muscles.

"Get in," I say.

His rolling eyes beneath his steamy glasses give the message of a Magic Eight Ball: *Very Doubtful*.

"It's not far," he moans.

"Get in," I insist.

He concedes, but he strains against the constraint of his seat belt as we drive into his neighborhood.

"Practice was the length it was for a reason," I say. "I don't want you to burn yourself out."

"OK, Ms. Pont," he groans.

He guides me through wide, clean streets. Children

on Big Wheels look up at the car and wave. Piles of bright leaves dot tidy lawns.

"Thank you," he says as I pull into the driveway of his house. "Thanks," he repeats as he hops from the car.

Through his expressions of gratitude, his impatience trickles.

He runs up the driveway, down the walk, to the front door of his house. He cuts no corners and finds his stride, savoring every step.

He acquired this desire to run on his own without coaching, cajoling, or the knowledge of Rajeev.

Friendship, in any form, begins with play. But, as it grows, it loses its need for games.

Once, when they were young, Nimish and Rejeev decided to brighten a white room. Standing on dressers, they painted rainbows, helping each other shove the dressers along the walls until the painting was complete.

Friendship, at first, defies the laws of physics, which would, if they prevailed, keep us circling each other like runners on a perpetual track. We are drawn to each other with a gravity that defies time and space.

But in the end, respecting the physical, affection sends us arcing into space toward some invisible finish line.

This is gravity's rainbow, and Nimish and Rajeev repaint it daily.

———

DURING A FREE PERIOD, I go to the cafeteria for coffee. Dave is there, tucked neatly into a seat at the back table near the door, elbows folded in, like a bird sleeping beneath his own wing. This space, a home to him and Sam George for four years of high school, is littered with their debris: Sam's black sweater, unloved math books, the crumbs of much-loved fast-food breakfasts, plastic gizmos, official documents, ugly ties. A library book is open before Dave, its plastic protective wrapping slightly oily. He looks up at me and reaches for his coffee.

With my coffee, I sit at another table. Dave approaches with a manila folder. From it, he pulls a poem.

He asks me to edit it, a poem about love and parting:

> I remember when
> the August was cut through with winter,
> when her eyes looked all tattered,
> and we sat on the edge of February.
> My suitcase was packed
> and we waited so long,
> like creaking stairs.

As I edit, I give him everything I have: one image and a sense of time. Now, the district race two weeks away, he understands what I mean. We speak the same blunt language of desire.

7. Seconds

In 864,000 seconds, a gunshot will signal the start of the District XI race.

Seconds are a difficult unit to grasp. Practice over, I ponder other seconds.

The mid-October sun sets a few seconds before suppertime.

The muscles in Gretchen and Leyla's legs when they walk away from practice, 5,184,000 seconds into the season, are outlined in blue shadows. Their taut arms swing slightly away from their torsos.

Though Oliver went back for seconds on pasta at lunch, he is starving now that practice is over. Lately, he has grown a couple inches. Knobby wrists protrude from the sleeves of his too-short shirt.

Samantha, corduroy legs swishing, runs down the path from the school building toward her mother's car. Six seconds from door to door. She hops in the passenger side, smiling, unwinded.

Dave, beginning a 21,600-second train ride through the autumn afternoon, is bound for a college in New England to measure his future.

Katie's haircut, 1,296,000 seconds old, has inched past elegance, too long to be short, too short to be long.

Tom, our second-place runner, has been loitering after practice, discussing the upcoming race against Warren Tech. Dave gone for a few days, he blinks to envision first in our second-to-last race before districts. He smiles modestly and slips away into the dusk.

Do we have too many or too few seconds? Have we used our seconds wisely? Will seconds logically lead to firsts? My mind is a chaos of questions, but my stopwatch can't answer any of them accurately until the district race is over.

Time is that which Tom and the rest desire as well as despise. Lately, it has seemed merciful, even friendly. It has altered them all because that is what time does. Nonetheless, they are awestruck by how much they have changed in two months. They feel the transformation in all the ways they move. There is a pleasure, a security, in knowing they feel no need to stop.

In anticipation of the state race, for which the top two teams and the top fourteen individuals qualify in the district race, I call a hotel in State College and reserve two rooms. Some—Samantha, Dave, maybe Leyla and Tom—just might make it; time has been that kind to them.

On second thought, I call back and reserve two more rooms, beds enough for all the girls and all the boys. I know that if I waste too much time, all the rooms will be taken.

THE DAY BEFORE THE RACE against Warren Tech, Sam George is back, wearing his black socks. The day's steady rain has just stopped, and the asphalt, like geodes, is sparkling and matte. Pulling water from shallow puddles, Sam and I mark patterns with the rubber treads of our sneakers as we wait for the others.

"How long is Dave staying at Brown?" I ask.

"Two days," he says. "But I'm worried he won't make it back." He thrusts his foot into shallow water and sends a burst of droplets up his bare calf.

I shrug, untroubled. Sam is worrying about a different Dave, the accidental poet, the one with whom he parted in September when he became injured.

The rest of the team gathers. To ward off the weather, they wear long-sleeved T-shirts and furry socks. Arms crossed, feet tapping to keep warm, they are quiet and subdued. I explain the workout: because the rain has soaked the grass of the cross country course, we'll loop three times along the driveway that figure-eights the campus.

As the crowd starts to move along the narrow road, a low giggle ripples through the quiet. Nimish and Rajeev look sideways over their glasses. Leyla weaves in and out of the pack. Samantha moves up next to Sam and sends him a complicitous glance.

Oliver starts it: in a pothole by the science labs, he jumps, hitting a deep, foamy puddle with two flat feet. A surge of grain-flecked water, double-pronged, soaks Sam and Samantha. Gretchen flees, finding a place to hide behind Katie and Kristy. Sam and Samantha stutter-step and turn on Oliver. Surrounding him, they jump up and down in a trough of water while he holds his hands over his face.

The war now on, the road ceases to be a road and becomes, instead, a series of tactical possibilities. Swiping at water with straight legs, Tom and Leyla are on the offensive, sending arcs toward a cowering band of freshmen. Pistonlike, Nimish and Rajeev work up a general shower over the center of the team. Eventually all of them stomp and splash, running ahead to stake out uncharted bodies of water, ruining their sneakers, missing their marks and dousing themselves, laughing until they can hardly breath enough to move, turning a run, an orderly process of getting from point A to point B, into utter chaos.

Finally, everyone gasps out their last laughs and falls into the set motions of their usual pace. They drift apart, scattering along the driveway in pairs or trios. I stay up front with Sam and Tom, who, exhilarated from playing in puddles, can't resist a brisker gait than a prerace workout requires. With long strides, they cruise down the driveway that leads to the gate of the school. Their legs and arms are painted with streaks of dirty water, their faces dabbed with lines of mud.

Sam begins to accelerate. Knowing better, Tom holds back. Sam hurtles away from us, his toes just touching pavement; he has been dormant so long, letting his ankle heal, that he can do nothing but relish the sense of flight. Continuing to speed up, he pulls farther and farther away from me and Tom. When Sam stops at the end of the third loop, he looks back, sees the distance between him and us, and nods.

When Tom and I finally reach Sam, I double over beside him, then look up. Sam's knuckles press into his pelvis. The corners of his mouth, turned down, cut lines to his chin. He breathes deep and calm, in and out, smooth and silent, in control of the rhythms of time.

As he and Tom walk away, I wonder if either will own tomorrow's race and, if so, who will have to live with second.

THE TEAM HAS TWO RACES to run one week before the district race. Because there is little they can do at this point in the way of training to shave more seconds off their times, they fantasize:

The voices over the loudspeaker echo (Laay-deees and genntelmin!) as if we are entering a striped circus tent. Bronze, gold, and crimson trees wave like royal banners. Runners, hundreds of them, are pretty horses, groomed and prancing (knees up; shoulders erect); coaches crack whips, twiddle their mustachios, and smile. Four different races thunder, Ben-Hur style, around Lehigh's cross country course (AA boys and girls, AAA boys and girls, fighting to the death) and it's the greatest show on earth, one ring better than a three-ring circus. Nero, Guinevere, and the King of Sweden all come forward at the end of the race to crown Moravian Academy with laurels.

Leyla and Oliver concede, Nimish and Rajeev concede, even Sam George concedes, that first place—as an idea or an actuality—is a fiction, a fantasy. But what about second?

More than anyone, Tom thinks these thoughts to himself as our bus jolts along the highway to New Jersey for the Warren Tech race. He sits up straight, knees apart, feet planted squarely on the slip-proof floor. Pressing his muscled shoulders into the green vinyl seat back, he lifts his straight nose to the open window. Thick fingers furrow his cornstalk hair. Ambitious to attend Cornell, he has worked diligently during his four years at Moravian Academy at many things—among them math, kung fu, Spanish, running. Tom understands the integrity of second, its singular place: just after first. It is as solid as the ground on which he runs.

The year before, to earn the rank of Eagle Scout, Tom worked long, solitary hours to set embankments, strip bushes, spread gravel, and pour a straight line of concrete on the saturated ground around Green Pond so that his team could race the course in any weather. From the shovel, trowel, and rake, his shoulders thickened. When, using his last name, we dubbed the well-laid path the "Haggerty Memorial Highway," the course became his.

But his ownership of our home course has been tenuous; those who place first in races vie for squatter's rights.

Now he has the chance to lay claim to the course at Warren Tech. When we arrive and dismount the bus in the back parking lot behind the school's auto shop, I approach him. His upper arms are as big as my thighs.

"This is your race, Tom," I say.

As he shakes his head slightly, looking down, his small mouth parts in a tiny smile.

We scramble up the hill behind the school to the cross country course. The afternoon is olive-colored. The grass, a little overgrown, is pale and spiky. Lost on the open field are lots of parents—Gretchen's mother, Kristy's father, Oliver's mother and father—holding their coats closed. No one tries to talk; they all seem too far away. Fists in pockets, they roam around to find the starting line, to establish a sense for the course, but they keep circling back to the place that they began.

After a team I had not expected, Belvidere, emerges from a bus and mounts the grassy plateau, a trio of Warren Tech runners walk us through the course: along the perimeter of the grounds, across the front of the building, then behind it in a zigzagging motion. Leyla and Gretchen get dizzy. Chatting to themselves, walking briskly, the Warren Tech runners start to lose us. We follow as best we can as the unmarked path twists and turns around the school, through a Christmas-tree farm, then around the school again. Though I try to explain the sequence of the course, my words become jumbled. Even to Tom, who has run here once before, there seems to be neither beginning nor end.

Tom and Sam George lead the team on a warm-up along the last half mile of the course. After they shed their jackets and wind pants, the boys and the girls line up with Warren Tech and Belvidere along a diagonal that cuts strangely across the field. Tom, in the number one position, looks down the line of runners, then out at the tangle of the course. At the first command, he sets his nose forward. The starting gun sounds hollow in the tarnished bowl of the sky.

Forty-five runners from Belvidere, Warren Tech, and Moravian Academy, all visible, move away from us, toward us, then away, toward us, then away. On the periphery of the grassy plateau I cheer and shout out times, then I move back to the center to cheer and shout again. Tom passes once, twice. The runners are so close, and then again so far, that it is difficult to know who is in first place and who is in last. Second place has no meaning whatsover. Tom passes by a third time.

As the runners find their way into the Christmas-tree farm, my fingers tighten on my stopwatch. Coaching cross country is different from other sports. I can't point and call to Tom "run here—first place" or "run there to break eighteen minutes" as if I were setting up a play. He has to work out the numbers of the race himself.

Several minutes of quiet pass. Then a straight line of runners emerges from the Christmas-tree farm and files along the front of the school. A Warren Tech runner has a clear lead, but Tom is battling with a Belvidere runner for second.

On the final hill, Tom is using his strong arms to

vault himself along. His forearms bulk and flatten; his biceps bulk and flatten. Nevertheless, he drops a few steps behind the Belvidere runner, crossing the finish line in third place.

But when Bryan and Sam George follow immediately behind him, it is clear that the numbers are in our favor; the boys are soundly beating both Warren Tech and Belvidere.

Tom smiles his tiny smile. What does second or third mean if his team has won? Wandering cheerfully around the center of the plateau, stepping clumsily with thick but tired legs, he is like a child taking his initial steps, regarding, for the first time, the world as his. With the others, he now owns this course.

Samantha, meanwhile, finishes. I rush to the line to confirm the time I believe my watch is giving me. Josh, writing down places, isn't sure; the Belvidere coach is too busy to speak; Tom, my assistant coach, is taking times on another part of the course.

Samantha, though, knows without looking. She walks toward the official timers, as if in a dream, and they assure her, warmly, yes, you broke twenty minutes by two seconds. Samantha turns to me, eyes wide. "Nineteen fifty-eight," I exclaim, wrapping my arms around her spare shoulders. Those two seconds mean so much more than simply winning; they mean she owns the race, and no one can take it from her.

Leyla and Gretchen cross the finish line amid much cheering. Arms hug; voices chirp and hoot. Oliver bolts frantically around to spectators and teammates exclaiming, "Can you believe it? Samantha broke twenty!"

Kristy and Katie, walking away from the line, have no problems believing it.

What's to believe about time? We have measured it enough to know its uniformity. It is human ability that requires belief, like Kristy's ability to gather the girls into a tight circle and tell them that they, as a team, have emerged from the chaos of the race and won.

When I was little, and my father, a football coach at Yale University, wrote X's and O's on a page, eleven per side, with arrows to signify motion, I was amazed by the orderliness of a play. Then, when I saw a game, I witnessed only chaos: all the X's looked the same, as did all the O's; there were no arrows on the field, only mud and fallen bodies. Yet, somehow, Yale scored, over and over, winning games, throughout the 1970s, for years on end.

After the games, when my father held out his stubbly cheek for me to kiss, I knew there must be order in chaos.

Today, we could not have anticipated the presence of Belvidere, nor the gift they gave us of another win. In this science of competition, there are so many variables that it all appears to be a muddle. Suddenly and not mathematically, in regular-season competition, disregarding invitationals, our boys' record is 8–2 and the girls' record is 5–1. Pressing hard on my clipboard, I write these figures out to make them real. I am glad I had not paused in the chaos of the season to tally the boys' victories over Perkiomen, Solebury, and the four teams they defeated at Belmont Plateau nor the girls' successes over Warren Hills, Solebury, and Pius before this race. With the addition of two more wins, they are ripe numbers.

I give them a second glance: 8–2, 5–1. On second thought, they are gorgeous numbers. They signify all that we can ask for at this second in time—hope.

Walking back to the bus, Gretchen nestles her head into Kristy's shoulder. Leyla hooks Katie's arm. Kate Webbink and Holly, losing their shyness, press to the center of the group. Samantha is at the heart of this body of girls, sharing ownership of the race with them all.

Tumbling into their seats, the girls are giddy, swishing and flirting as if they were little girls smoothing down party clothes with little hands. Wearing their new muscles, Leyla, Gretchen, and Samantha have forgotten how young they, in fact, are. Clinging to the seats of the school bus, they are as excited as children who have, for the first time, jumped and splashed in the deep end of a pool: they shake slightly, from cold and shock, nervous in the breadth of their pleasure.

Kristy, the mother at the front of the bus, is turning around, but not to scold them. She wants them to jump back into the deepest end: the district race.

———

CONTRARY TO SAM'S WARNINGS, Dave returns safely from his college trip on Friday, confident that Brown is his second choice. He is wearing his T-shirt emblazoned with the Superman logo, the decal pale and slightly furry.

I have designed a workout with Dave in mind. Though the rest of the team is tapering, in need of a little speed work and no more distance, Dave requires, one more time, to remind himself what it's like to race five kilometers. He has not run that distance in 604,800 seconds, and will run it in the district race 518,400 seconds from now.

So we caravan to the cross country course on Lehigh University's mountaintop campus, the site of the district race. There, I set up the workout: I divide the group into teams of three, each leg running a mile or so apiece, except Dave, who will run the distance.

As we are stretching, he asks, "This workout is for me?"

"It's for the rest of the team, too," I assure him. "Monday we're going to run Jim Thorpe in a three-person relay, just like this."

But, as if he were running a real race, he feels pressure to earn his ownership.

I run on a team with Tom and a lacrosse player I recruited for the event. At the mile mark, I wait with the second legs of the other teams. After Dave passes, a hundred yards behind him the lacrosse player appears. When he slaps my hand, I am off.

Up a hill, then down, I squint in the sunshine at Dave's dark outline. Slowly, I gain on him. He glances over his shoulder. Though I am terrified to catch him, afraid of what it will mean, I do not slow down. I want Dave to keep racing.

Another hill. I am ten yards behind him. My mouth is dry. My shoulder is throbbing. I fight with a devil in my head who tempts me to slow down.

Finally, Dave shakes me around the periphery of a cornfield. Significantly behind Dave, I reach for Tom, who is waiting patiently for the touch of my hand.

Though when I stop I am breathing uneasily, noisily, I cannot keep from smiling. I jog to the finish, still wheezing, and watch Dave's strong finish, the slight bounce in his sprint, and Tom in second, feet close to the ground as he comes down the final slope.

After the other teams have completed the relay, I describe our cool down: the last portion of the course. I want everyone to think about how they run it, the gradual uphill through the cornfields, the sharp downhill out of the trees, the rise by the football stadium, then the long decline to the finish line. It is a mile that requires strategy as well as toughness. This part of the practice is for Samantha; she needs to consider the course carefully, to make it her own.

While I am talking, Oliver pulls out a lollipop and pops it into his mouth.

I promptly take it from him and suck on it myself.

Rajeev leans over to Nimish and asks, "Did she *actually* put that in her mouth?"

"She actually did," reports Nimish.

"Gross," Rajeev concludes emphatically.

"Doh!" Oliver says, reaching out. I hand the lollipop over, but Oliver has taken the hint. He rewraps it and tucks it into the pocket of his shorts. He starts the cooldown run with Dave and Tom. Samantha and I follow more slowly, talking seriously about the terrain, about the other teams who will be there, about how she is feeling.

As I come out of the cornfield with Samantha, so strong beside me, I see Oliver jogging along, his lollipop back in his mouth.

While we load the cars up to drive back to school, I try not to give Oliver a reproachful look, but I can't help myself. In order for us to make it to states, to even perform respectably at districts, fourteen people must run seriously. The likelihood of my coaching them all into that alignment seems impossible. What with lollipops, puddles, and the intricacies of personality, there are too many variables; when I imagine the math, the quantity of seconds, I see only chaos.

BECAUSE OF THE SATS on Saturday, we were forced to change the date of the Jim Thorpe race to Monday,

259,200 seconds before the district race. As a result, the Jim Thorpe coach and I modified the race; instead of the standard 3.1-mile distance, it will be a three-person-team relay. The shorter distance will be less of a strain on bodies primed for the districts.

But my mom and dad, who planned to watch the race in Jim Thorpe on Saturday, don't change their plans. Saturday night they check into an inn and meet me for dinner right on time.

When I was little, we would stop at fancy restaurants on our way home from my father's football games, sometimes with the team, sometimes with my parents' friends. We sat at long tables with cloth napkins folded into fans and pats of butter shaped like flowers. My mother always scolded me, telling me not to fill up on bread, but I couldn't resist, the bread was so soft and I was so hungry. So when my fancy-restaurant chicken came in its heavy sauce, I was never a bit hungry.

In Jim Thorpe, I am careful not to fill up on bread. I wait calmly for my shrimp, asking my parents about family, friends, and their travels out West. When my shrimp arrives, I eat it slowly, asking about the dog and the cat between bites.

I am the second child, and though I have never quite been entirely sure what that, psychologically, was supposed to mean, I think it has something to do with an inability to focus, to follow through, to do the right thing. I am proud of myself for having broken the pattern by eating my meal so carefully.

But I leave that restaurant wishing, deep down, that I had filled up on the bread. It looked so warm and soft.

Though I am disappointed when my parents leave on Sunday morning, I know they came to see me, not the race. They are so deeply woven into the pattern of my life that they can't understand how important my runners are to me.

"WHEN ARE WE LEAVING for Jim Thorpe?" Nimish and Rajeev ask Monday morning. As the teams are going to race in the relay format we used at Lehigh on Friday— teams of three individuals each running a mile apiece— they see the race as a game.

"Yesterday," I say.

"*Hoo-hoo!*" they shout, Homer Simpson–like, understanding me, knowing they will leave so early that, missing most of the school day, they will be allowed to play and play.

Though we arrive unnecessarily early, the day is silky. We lounge in the tall grass by Lake Mauch Chunk, the location of the Jim Thorpe course, greedily drinking up fall's last sunshine. Most of the senior boys, Sam Cohen, Dave, and Tom, confer about an advanced physics test they have tomorrow. Nervous, Sam grills Dave and Tom for quick solutions to a problem about the force of a spoon leaning against the edge of a salad bowl. While Dave tries to explain his unorthodox solution, Tom just chuckles, unable to put in words that which is so evident to him.

Sam usurps my clipboard, flips over stats from an early race, and draws a symbol for Oliver: a curve of a head with a loop at the top to indicate the samurai hair Oliver sports for races. Inspired, Sam reduces everyone else on the team to their lowest level. Tom's, a karate headband on a smiling face, is most accurate. Looking over Sam's shoulder, Tom nods approvingly.

Sam keeps drawing until everyone on the team has a symbol. It is a long, complex alphabet that doesn't, in the end, add up to anything.

A team I had not expected, Panther Valley, emerges from a bus and scrambles down the grassy slope to the lake. The bodies it carries, wrapped in black and gold, are not Belvidere. Panther Valley, a school in the coal region, is fabled for its athletics.

Finally a bus arrives full of Jim Thorpe's red, white, and blue uniforms. Three of their runners lead Moravian and Panther Valley on a walk of the course, which travels deep into the woods.

"So, how does your team look?" I ask the Panther Valley coach.

"My girls are pretty good," he says.

A group is walking in front of us. They have gold

bows in their black hair, matching their black-and-gold uniforms. That detail, I know, can mean only one thing: they know just how fast they are.

When I drop back to join Samantha, Gretchen, and Leyla, they crowd together, rubbing shoulders like little girls sharing a secret. "If you girls win," I whisper, leaning in, "I'll take you to lunch at the Plaza Hotel."

They brighten, knowing the Plaza from *Eloise,* and they scamper off, eager to make this race their own. But, seeing the Panther Valley boys hover uncomfortably at the back of the group walking the course, I suspect this is a race for the boys, too.

"This is your race," I say to Tom, who has earned the spot as second leg of our top relay, the one who must maneuver the lonely woods by himself.

He offers his tiny smile, then he, Leyla, and the other second-leg runners head to the mile mark in the heart of the woods.

When the first runners of the relay teams, Gretchen and Sam George among them, vanish into the woods, I do not see them again. At home and on nearly all other courses, the runners draw along the watchers; we drift behind like pilgrims, grateful for a privileged view at measured moments: the mile mark, the two-mile mark. Though I try to imagine, I do not know what struggles Gretchen, Sam, Leyla, and Tom undergo, what battles they win. I attempt to envision the race in my mind based on what I know about the runners and what I know about time, but the vision is scrambled by the whirling motion of leaves.

There is, in fact, no real race, just a flickering motion through the trees. Dave, Samantha, and the other third-leg runners loiter, eyeing chicken, chips, and promising Tupperware spread on a nearby picnic bench. I am glad my parents aren't there. They would be watching nothing.

Sam has been gone several minutes, and the birds are settling into evening. I dislodge a pebble from the ground. At last, from a deep hollow in the trees, the Jim Thorpe boy emerges, tags his teammate, then falls away into shadows. Tom follows, in second place, reaching for Dave, who takes what Tom has to give and is off.

Two Panther Valley girls, thick, dark hair shot through with gold ribbons, touch the hands of their teammates. Behind them, maple hair and birch skin, Leyla is, as she comes through the trees, barely visible. Samantha reaches a hand back for her, pulling. Then she runs off to fight with time.

Quiet, as if running on air, Dave appears along the dirt path by the lake. Everyone flutters to gather at the finish line. No one anticipated just how fast Dave would reappear. Except me. He crosses the line in a full sprint.

Along the dirt path, the Panther Valley girls maintain their lead. I see Samantha, several yards back, unsmiling, battling time along the dirt path. There is too much of it between her and the Panther Valley girls to take on. When she walks away from the finish line, she doesn't look at anyone.

As we head back to the bus, I assure Samantha and the girls that they will find another time to earn a visit to the Plaza Hotel.

In the darkness of the bus, they fantasize about the Plaza while I plan the pasta I will cook for them at my friend Peter's house the night before the state race in State College—the race they run once they've been successful at districts—a chaos of noodles in a muddle of sauce, and I suddenly wish I could go back to that night before the first race and make everyone eat more, could say something inspiring, could pump cleaner oxygen into the air for them to breathe.

Time, though, doesn't give us second chances. So we'll have to run districts as we are.

Really, that has been true all along. Two months has not made Leyla, Oliver, and the others new; it has only exaggerated the qualities they always possessed, from the time they were thoughts in their parents' heads. They expand in fractal patterns, iterating, over and over, the exact same qualities, so that even in the chaos of their actions, there is order.

TUESDAY, 172,800 SECONDS before districts, Sam is wearing his black socks. Tapering for the district race,

Sam and the rest run easy. Without much chatter or antics from Nimish and Rajeev, practice ends in half an hour.

While the rest of the team scatters, Samantha, as I instructed, appears from the school building. Because she has never run the full course at Lehigh University, I told her to miss practice so I could take her there and talk her through it. Lingering when he sees Samantha, Sam overhears our plan. He volunteers to tag along, promising to drive Samantha home.

Flanked by Sam and Samantha, I explain the terrain of the course: the second mile is the hardest; you can win in the third mile. Sam drops a little behind me, pulling Samantha back with a nod to confer with her about what I am saying and to convey privately what I'm not. As we jog, we form a neat triangle, moving in unison while the crickets sing.

Because Sam knows this course, having run in the district race three times before, and because he cares about Samantha, they are a full second behind me. Second is not always lesser than first, nor first greater than second. Numbers seldom fall in an orderly pattern. Running at this moment, the three of us cannot see the pattern we make because we are inside it.

When we finish our run, Samantha knows the course. Sam has given it to her.

Time brings muscle, but it brings entropy, too. As I

drive back from Lehigh, alone and tired, I imagine the team—and our hopes—randomly scattered:

Tom, breaking a cement block with the side of his hand, steps back, astonished. He can't believe what he's done; he doubts he will do it again. He smiles and looks away modestly.

Katie folds her sheaves of hair into a girlish ponytail.

Dave, wandering through the autumn night, reaching for leaves, stumbling over roots, loses his way.

Samantha, standing on her front stoop with Sam, is afraid to move, afraid to smile.

Oliver, at his family's dinner table, pokes at his vegetables. He asks, petulantly, if he can be excused.

The muscles in Gretchen's and Leyla's legs, nestled on couches, lose their blue shadows; their loose arms dangle over piles of cushions.

The late-October sun has set long ago, and I, cutting off my imaginings, shiver home through a brittle night, a few seconds away from suppertime. I will fill up on bread, trying to convince myself that the 162,000 seconds left till the gunshot sounds for the district race are neither too much nor too little time left to prepare us to run faster than we have ever run before.

8.   Superheroes

The day before the district race, the team forms a sloppy circle on the uneven ground. Kristy, taking charge, is wearing a Superman T-shirt, long-sleeved to ward off the cold. The shirt is electric blue, so bright it could be neoprene or kryptonite. "Arms over your head!" she commands, her freckled face set and uncompromising. Everyone complies. "Other side!" she dictates. Though arms move slowly, Kristy jostles them along, bouncing through the first stretches, the pattern comfortably memorized.

They are pulling on their quadriceps, standing on one foot and gripping the toe of their other foot from behind. Pointing at Kristy's shirt with his free hand, Rajeev queries, "Isn't that *Dave's* symbol?" He wobbles on his foot, swimming through air with his one free hand to keep his balance.

"On your backs!" instructs Kristy.

Dave, on the far side of the circle, remarks, "I think DC Comics would have a different opinion." He smiles, showing his gums, before finding the ground with his shoulder blades.

Disinterested in symbols, Kristy shrugs off questions and discussion. "On your stomachs," she barks. Flipping over, the group lifts arms and feet into the air, forming strained arcs with their bodies that require all their intensity to maintain. In Dave's neck, the muscles tighten into wicklike ribbons.

"OK," Kristy grants.

Relieved and heaving, they collapse, face down. It is a cold day with ropes of wind snapping in all directions, even along the ground. Just a few frizzled leaves soften the trees. The bony branches expose a sickly light.

As the team continues stretching, cajoled by Kristy, everyone fidgets, struggling with thoughts of the world outside the circle. In school, it is the end of the marking period; symbols and patterns to be memorized for tests and quizzes, as well as phantom grades—A, B, and F—

float through the soupy air. Papers, projects, corrections, notebooks, bibliographies, apologetic notes from parents, and, for some, college applications are due. As Dave, Nimish, and Gretchen ring trees to press against the flaking bark and stretch their shins, they face others without seeing, pull on their legs without feeling. Along with the late-October cold, life is prickling and numbing them.

Leyla, particularly, is mummied in thought. She stands before a tree, forgetting its purpose. Her mother is sick again. In her face, her features cluster together. When a nudge of wind jostles Leyla awake, she dutifully follows Kristy's motions.

To keep muscles from tightening, they hurriedly begin their run. Dave steps gingerly over knobs of dead grass and lozenges of frozen mud while Gretchen dodges them, side to side. Frozen patches mottle the Haggerty Memorial Highway. On the lacrosse field, a hundred geese reluctantly flap away to create a narrow path for the runners. On the driveway, cars move toward them, unable to see through the sepia light.

After one lap of hazards, they are glad to stop.

Working through sets of sprints, acceleration slows. Shoulders grumble and legs complain. Gretchen, annoyed with her rebellious appendages, tries to use her back to pull her through. When her spine joins the naysayers, she calls on her lungs. When they, too, bow out, she reaches for her heart. As I call for one final sprint, she looks at me, frightened; she doesn't know how much of herself she has left. But she finds some muscles and a ligament or two that have not jumped ship.

To conclude practice, we stretch again in the warmth of the auditorium, Sam George leading. He speaks in soothing tones. He lingers in the stretches that require reclining, taking sport with Oliver, who turns it on the freshmen, who, in turn, long for the arbitrary power their high school future offers. Laughing, comfortable, everyone relaxes on the all-weather carpet, forgetting their worries, solidifying into singular selves.

How much of themselves do they need to leave behind tomorrow in order to qualify for states? The demands are difficult to calculate. Everything and everyone against which they struggle become a nemesis, wielding fantastic weapons and spewing fatalistic comments. In the district race, they will confront twenty-six teams in the girls' race, twenty-five in the boys', from the Lehigh Valley, the northern coal region, and mysterious towns farther west, nearly as far as Three Mile Island. How many of these winged foes can they combat at once while they, too, try to mount the air?

For me, the 8–2, 5–1 records of boys and girls resonate with a symbolism not unlike Superman's flashy *S*. They suggest that Dave, Nimish, Leyla, and Gretchen have each divided, as if by mitosis, into two people: person and persona. The person is distracted, doubting, possesses sinuses, wears Band-Aids; the persona is Runner, undiluted, focused on forward motion, conscious of how awesome they are when watched.

They all feel, though, as they did in mid-August, neither more nor less themselves.

Which of us is right? Have they changed a little or not at all? Who can tell—they cannot see themselves from the outside, as I can, and I cannot see them from within.

As they leave practice and enter the thought-filled night, they name the more palpable villains in their minds, personifying them—Chemistry Test, English Paper, Spanish Oral—with pockmarked faces, tentacles, and merciless laughs. In the darkening sky, Venus, an orange pore just above the horizon, is joined by more celestial bodies that Dave, Nimish, and Gretchen cannot name, leaking a light that is both stark and overwhelming.

Still sitting, Leyla is alone in the orange light of the auditorium, her tiny legs brushing the spongy carpet, as if preparing to combat all arch rivals and fears at once: home, school, and Lehigh University's cross country course which, in her memory, seems to, in fact, cross the entire country.

She needs to leave, but she doesn't feel up to fighting three leviathans at once. When Kristy goes to her, reaching out a hand, Leyla hesitates before she takes it.

———

THE NEXT MORNING is bright and quiet, as if the battles the night before were a fantasy. During third period, just in time for this afternoon's race, T-shirts arrive. Grinning, Dave, Sam George, and Samantha pluck them from folded piles and try them on. They are white with electric blue rings around collar and cuff. A toothpaste tube, in the same shade of blue, marks the front, an arbitrary symbol concocted by Dave. Bemused, the younger runners study this new uniform before they pull them over their heads. They look around, wondering whether the shirt transforms them in other people's eyes. So much of a superhero, they know, is in the uniform.

For the younger runners, though, nothing seems to change. They are exactly who they were in mid-August. Nevertheless, in their estimation, as in mine, the same is not true for the varsity. As a result, on the bus to Lehigh, the group of younger runners trembles with excitement over the show they will see in the District XI race at Lehigh University from their heroes Dave, Gretchen, and the other twelve who will run today.

Gretchen is pressed tight against a window in the back of the bus, her red wind jacket zipped high so that the white-lined hood plumps in an arc behind her head.

Nimish, across from her, jacket loose to expose the blue-ringed neck of his T-shirt and the blue-shadowed skin of his neck, is humming to himself.

Have they changed a little or not at all?

Only the stopwatch can tell.

When the bus drops us off near the starting line of the race, we see Liberty High School's encampment: blankets, coolers, and a legion of bodies. The Liberty girls look like Valkyries in their undergarments. The Liberty boys, in reflective sunglasses, look like Spiderman, Captain America, and the Riddler.

We stake out our own territory, spreading our motley array of jackets and jugs to claim ownership of a patch of ground. The younger runners—John, Rachel, Sara, and Vinayak—in jeans, leather shoes, and Moravian Academy jackets, circle like cats, trying to make the place comfortable.

Only the top seven on the girls' and boys' teams run at districts. Though seven ran in the varsity races of the invitationals, there was always a race for all the junior varsity, so top seven did not seem, at the time, quite so selective. Now, however, it is more than selective; it is an acknowledgment of superhuman powers.

The younger runners, perched on the low wooden fence between the road and the wide expanse of grass, look on, some with awe, some with envy. From that vantage point, everything—the silver sky, the line of trees, the open spaces, the football stadium, the number of runners—seems colossal. The smell of hot dogs explodes above. Speakers, set high on poles, squeal arcane, plaintive announcements.

"District XI T-shirts are available at the registration table!" "Coaches, please be sure your runners do not wear hats!" "First call, Boys' AA!"

Everyone tingles, hearing the race is soon, and the adulation slowly brings Dave into focus. He is standing away from the fence, away from everyone, wholly absorbed in the chewing of a nail. He raises his thick eyebrows as if he is tasting something new.

The younger runners nod to each other: that is Dave, their Superman. "It's freezing," the younger runners exclaim, pulling their jackets around them. Incredulous, they watch athletes from other teams who parade, unperturbed by the air, in colored wind suits that are buoyant as balloons. Before their awe and jealousy shift camps, they look back at Dave, still gnawing steadily at his nail, and Samantha, smiling at nothing. The younger runners snap their gaze back to Dave, then to Samantha, unprepared for these feelings of wonderment, discomfort, and childish anticipation.

Only Kristy is prepared for the cold with a duffel full of various gloves and hats. When she offers to share, the younger runners reach out greedily. The varsity boys, though, wave them away. Preoccupied, they haven't taken the time to notice the cold.

But they regain their presence of mind to find the bathrooms.

As they wander back from the stadium to our encampment, in singles and in pairs, they pause and exchange words with friends past and present who stop them along the way, but mostly they are quiet. The desire to do well enough today to go to states robs them of words. They are lost inside themselves. In their minds, they work to construct who they will be for the race that begins in fifteen minutes.

After their warm-up run, the varsity boys find their place on the line, near the center, followed by a stream of parents and younger runners. The team next to us, sprinting off the line, jumping up and down to keep their legs loose, is completely uniform, right down to their *Top Gun* jawlines and scratchy crew cuts. Our boys—Dave, Tom, Sam George, Oliver, Bryan, Sam Cohen, and Nimish— have let go some of their fear and are shaking, grinning, and chattering with their friends. Nimish is now singing to himself, shuffling in place and rubbing his hands together. Dave is still chewing on that tenacious nail.

The good guys all need to change, somehow, in order to become superheroes: Clark Kent pulls open his starched white shirt to reveal his electric-blue suit; Green Lantern exposes his ring to his essential lantern. Anger, danger, and the desire for revenge provoke them to change who they are into who they should be. The potential that lies within them is realized simply by the desire to do so.

The other teams continue to sprint, to stretch, to

shake loose their snakelike legs: only villains—like the Penguin or Lex Luthor—maintain their identity one hundred percent of the time. Our team, in contrast, will wait for the proper moment before they undergo their metamorphosis, so the younger runners think.

The official shouts. A hush falls. While coaches and spectators drop back to a respectful distance, 159 runners form a thick line. Dave and Nimish, a few feet apart, look up, down at their feet, up, and down again. Nimish brushes a toe along the painted white line as if testing the temperature of water.

When the gun sounds, a roar accompanies the flood of runners surging up the shallow slope to the stadium. We all look for Dave, Nimish, and the others, waiting for them to shuck their white tanks and red shorts to reveal their greater personas, but we cannot pick them out in the mass of remarkably similar bodies.

Within the flurry of runners, in a hushed bubble, Dave is moving a little too slowly. His lower back is burning; his thighs won't lift his knees. He is distracted, digging: underneath his flimsy uniform, underneath one layer of chamois-colored skin, Dave thinks he will find someone other than himself who moves in a violet blur. While other runners pass him near the peak of the grassy incline, he tenses, as if struggling to find that persona.

In the mob behind Dave, Nimish is no longer singing. Tight in his own stifling bubble, he is waiting to explode from within and finish the race in an instant. His legs feel small and heavy simultaneously. His glasses begin to steam. He keeps running, waiting for the change.

As the shrinking, thinning flow of competitors trickles around the left turn by the stadium, we watch, feeling weak, wishing Dave would dodge behind a tree, change his identity, and save us.

But Dave, who has just made the initial left turn, can't find the knob, lever, or rip cord that, when twisted, flipped, or pulled causes him to realize another identity. He passes markers signaling one kilometer, one mile. The pain in his back has swallowed itself, and his thighs are more cooperative. He ceases his internal search, accepting that he must run as himself.

Behind Dave, Nimish, throat and shoulders blotched with cherry heat, still has not found his stride. But after the noise dies and the crowd thins, at the left turn past the stadium, the mist over Nimish's goggle-like glasses clears. He finds himself locked in a fold of boys, all much taller than he is. In front of them flicker other jerseys. Though he isn't sure how far he has gone, or how far he has to go, he tries to pick up his pace. As he lifts his knees up and his elbows back, they crackle like lit matches.

He can't gain momentum. He is up against something much bigger than himself. Blades of grass on the side of the path are razors; branches reach with suction cups. In a moment, the gang of boys has him locked into place, and he races inside them, wondering if they are friend or foe.

At the halfway mark, in the long stretch before the uphill into the cornfield, thousands of people cheer. Dave, gray and vacant-eyed, looks neither left nor right. His elbows press tightly into his ribs, his body knotted, his feet flat to the ground. This, too, is a part of Dave.

A minute and a half later, Nimish passes. He is still locked into his place; like Dave he looks neither left nor right. As the girls and I call to him, though, we see just a hint of elastic spring, just a shadow of a smile. Those signs are all we need to know that Nimish is himself.

While Dave is emerging from the cornfield, the top competitors, from Palmerton, Northern Lehigh, and North Schuylkill, are opening their strides, their legs sharp and quick as dueling sabers, for the finale.

A minute later, entering the long, cord-lined quarter mile to the finish, Dave musters his characteristically explosive sprint. His thin legs, downed with hair, turning round with the quickness of a wheel, are a violet blur. Crossing the line with a time of 18:53, over a minute shy of what he expected, waiting in the long queue of finishers for the scorekeepers to write down numbers, he is still but jittery. With his teeth, he finds, again, his obstinate nail.

Nimish finishes two minutes and twenty-seven seconds later, his wide feet turned out in a floppy but strong finale. His time, 21:20, is one of his best for the season, outstanding for so difficult a course and for Nimish. In the chute, he resumes his hum.

Though Dave and Nimish ran at the same time, on the same course, they did not run the same race. The expectations, from within and from without, were wholly different. Even still, they ran races other than those they would have run yesterday or would run tomorrow. They ran races true only to themselves at that moment.

As a team, the boys finish seventeenth, their worst showing in recent years. Most of them are disappointed with their times and places, especially the seniors, Dave, Tom, and the Sams. But as they wander through the field by the finish line and the striped officials' tent, past other runners who finished before them and behind them, they feel strangely elated. They pull sweatshirts and jackets over their clammy skin, congratulating Nimish, and eager to watch the girls' race. Any desire they might have felt to go to states now appears false. As they walk to the starting line, that symbol of dread just thirty minutes earlier has transformed into a site of encouragement, camaraderie, even joy.

The younger runners don't understand. They wanted Dave and the others to live up to all the myths constructed around them and save the day. Myths explain the unexplainable, and, when they are deflated, they leave a void. So the younger runners walk, dejected, to the stadium to buy candy and soda.

Kristy, meanwhile, leads the girls on their warm-up run, seeking out the Stonehenge-like sculptures on the far side of the field. As the girls move side by side in an even line, arms nearly touching, they decrease in size until they are Bergman silhouettes dancing atop the landscape. Then they vanish. After what seems like a long time, they reappear, in that same line, facing us with unblinking eyes, ready to earn their place, as a team, in the state race.

The girls' race about to begin, the younger runners hurriedly return from the stadium with arms full of snacks and cheeks smeared with chocolate. Renewed, they turn the focus of their adulation on Samantha. But she is gone, melded into the larger body that Kristy holds together. So the younger runners, looking elsewhere, espy Leyla, who is tying the driftwood locks of her hair into a ponytail, pulling them out, then tying them back again. She is beside herself with nervous energy.

Ecstatic, eager for more, the younger runners look also to Gretchen, who is talking quietly to her mother in a separate sphere of untrodden grass and cloudless sunshine. Gretchen's face glows in the bone-pale light.

"Second call, Girls' AA!" the loudspeaker sputters over the steady wind.

One hundred sixty-five girls crowd the infield, moving as deliberately as the hundreds of thousands of Muslims who make the hajj to Mecca and the millions of Hindus who dive in the Ganges each year. Their entourages follow them with sweatshirts, cameras, and flattery. Our top seven—Samantha, Leyla, Gretchen, Holly, Kristy, Katie, and Kate Webbink—in their slot on the line, entertain friends, family, the younger runners, and the varsity boys, who, their race reduced to memory, are gregarious, high on air. As the girls giggle at Sam George's antics, they strip off their outer layers. With smooth arms and legs exposed to the cold, each is like the little mermaid on a rock in Copenhagen. Their fingers graze each other's arms as they step to the line.

When the official calls, hugs ensue, then everyone but the girls drops back. While parents close their eyes, friends tighten fists, and coaches dispel their obsession with numbers, trying telepathically to convey warm thoughts to those about to race, the younger runners cross their arms. They are a grizzly audience, impatiently waiting for earthquakes, thunder, and the emergence of superheroes.

The gun, though, makes the tiniest pop. The voices of fans, crying out every word of encouragement they can conceive, crackle like static. As the singular mass of girls flows up the slope toward the stadium, it offers up no burgeoning bodies, no wings, no capes, no forces to contend with that aren't, simply, a girl with swinging hair and skinny arms.

But the younger runners are willing to wait. While the rest of the spectators scatter, positioning themselves at strategic places along the course so they can witness moonlike crescents of the race, the younger runners pass Gummi Bears and Coke, spectating more than is observable by the average eye.

After Leyla makes the left turn by the stadium, she

finds herself behind a group of gilt bodies, among them the dark ponytail of a Panther Valley runner against whom she competed three days before. Leyla's sternum, her tiny hips, her moonstone knees swoon in their desire to blow past that girl like a kiss. She musters up her courage and closes her eyes.

Gretchen, just behind her, makes that left turn by the stadium. She glances left and right to see if anyone is watching her. Though her arms and feet feel thick, Gretchen's mind blooms with deep impulses to be strong, to be fabulous, and to be seen that way. She runs faster, using appendages and arteries that put up no fight, but open and contract like the bellows of an organ. She passes a runner, one flies by her, but then Gretchen draws closer to another.

Finding pleasure in the pain of running, she feels no need at all to change.

Though still in front of Gretchen, Leyla's desire misfires, and she is slowing down.

At the top of a rise, Leyla is besieged with anger: How could her own desire so betray her? How could she slow herself down? She struggles to pull herself together.

Moving into an opening of clear light, Gretchen sees Leyla running in front of her. Holly, knuckles and elbows cleft from tightness, sees Leyla. Forgetting about the rebellions within, they move toward each other, forming an isosceles triangle, Leyla at its apex. They cling to the pattern, adapting the lengths of the strides, finding that strength is not a comic-book force at all, but simple emotion.

At the halfway point, thousands of fans crying themselves hoarse, Leyla, Gretchen, and Holly hear familiar voices call their names, but they do not bother looking left or right. All the encouragement they need is among them. Gretchen assumes the peak of their formation.

As Samantha fights through her last mile to earn the right to run in the state race, glaring at Wilson and Notre Dame uniforms that dominate the route in front of her, Leyla, Gretchen, and Holly work their way through the cornfield, reconfiguring based on one another's needs. Leyla, sensing the end, acts as pacesetter for the other two.

Two minutes after Samantha crosses the finish line, Gretchen, Leyla, and Holly enter the final long, cord-lined quarter mile. As they begin to sprint, they spread across the wide avenue, as intense as they were in their warm-up run. Stepping forward, Gretchen finds the finish first. Her time—23:35—is her own, and her race is shared with her teammates.

Who are Gretchen and Leyla, really? Do they keep identities secret from us? When, after waiting through the long queue to get their places, Gretchen falls into her mother's arms and Leyla into mine, I sense there are no secrets. In running the best they could, they let themselves be known.

In the grassy area beside the finish chute and the race officials' tent, the assembling crowds take on the air of partygoers. Though some runners are crying, unable to be consoled, and other runners are falling, unable to stand, and still others are complaining, unable to make peace, most are flushed and smiling. Our seven girls, knowing the team placed ninth, their best finish in the history of Moravian Academy, by far, are giddy. Any desire they might have felt to go to states, as individuals or as a team, is irrelevant, now, in light of how well they ran. The director of our school works through the crowd and shakes hands all around, enclosing little fingers in his muscled palms. Friends pass through and offer Twizzlers. Sam George pays homage with deep bows. Even the younger runners, who did not see the races they imagined, join the revelry.

I am the outsider. For me, the party won't begin until I am certain that Samantha made it to states. There is a slim chance, and I cling to it.

As the sun sets, the festive atmosphere wanes. Mothers and fathers in their parkas drive away in their minivans to prepare supper. Though the younger runners are cold and hungry, I make them wait by the grandstand for the individual results of the girls' AA race. Generating their own warmth, the varsity boys and girls sit together on the ground, nearly on top of one another. They rock back and forth in rhythmic waves. Holly's face dances with laughter over the exchanges between Dave and Sam George.

Finally, an official appears with a pile of papers. My hand shakes as I take one. The ink is so faint I can hardly read the columns of numbers. I check them over again and again, pointing my chewed finger from the top of the list to the twenty-second spot.

The math keeps coming out the same: Samantha is two places away from making it to states.

As I wave everyone toward the bus, I can't look anyone in the eye. I'm too afraid I'll cry. Walking as fast as I can, I yammer to myself, why do we bother to run? What does it get us? Do we run to impress people? To please people? Who? Those who are too hard on us? Those who are too easy? Those we wish would care? Ourselves?

None of the above, I fume as I walk faster and faster. There is no reason to run. It's too hard. Too painful. Too absurd.

I know I'm about to cry.

I feel that the whole season has come to an abrupt end, that the fall was wasted, that none of us are good enough to be today's hero, let alone tomorrow's. The thought of a tomorrow makes me nauseous.

Though I am walking as fast as I can, Kristy catches me. "That was really good," she says. "That's a great start."

That's the *end*, I want to say, but I do not correct her. I can't talk; I'm certain I'm about to cry.

"We'll win leagues," she assures me, then, uninterested in a response, lapses into her own thoughts. She is planning strategy: formations and transformations. Tomorrow, for her, the season begins all over again. The foes of today will rise up, uglier, and she will, with the others, combat them. We have time. We have one race left.

"We'll win leagues," she repeats, as if it's the only logical conclusion to any line of questioning I might fire at her.

I stifle tears that well up for a new reason: I completely believe in her. I entrust Kristy to carry us on her back through the last week, through the league race, and into the arms of winter with trophies in hand.

Finally, I hide within the vinyl of the front seat of the bus and cry.

Around me, aluminum foil crackles like fire as the baked goods make their way from seat to seat. The satisfied quiet of biting, chewing, swallowing, and biting again fills the bus. Unburdened of the strong emotions Kristy gave me, I reach back for a cookie I made myself.

Looking from seat to seat at the mussed hair, the limp arms, the gray crescent moons beneath the eyes, and the girls crowded together in a private joke, I think: I've been watching all wrong. People don't go through mitosis. They don't keep personas behind glass for emergency situations. The goals I set for Dave and Samantha came from my imagination. So I couldn't savor the victories of Nimish, Leyla, Gretchen, and the rest of the girls.

Now, with Kristy, I've got my sights set on the Penn-Jersey Championship. I imagine that we'll win, and I pray my vision isn't obscured, once again, by my imagination.

9. Running on Air

On Saturday morning, quiet even for November, as I am tying the laces of my running shoes, the ringing of my phone cuts through the still air.

I know who it is: someone who wants to weasel out of practice.

"Ms. Pont do we *have* to run?" It is Sam George, his voice viscous from lack of sleep, with Samantha, Dave, and Bryan a dissonant chorus in the background. Sam is the spokesperson not only because he is the most charismatic but also because he is the least interested in running this morning, though not by much. Everyone on the team by now, early November, has exhausted their physical and mental fuel supplies and is running on little more than air.

"We were up all night, Ms. Pont," he says.

I imagine them watching movies in the dark under itchy blankets, huddled for warmth on a hardwood floor, tickling each other with their voices. "Come if you want," I say. "But promise you'll run sometime later today."

He is silent. "Just a minute."

I hear discussion in the background, voices, faint but distinguishable as if written in pen and rubbed out with an eraser. As I wait, I double-knot the laces of my shoes. They are frayed, and the patterned nubs of the soles are worn nearly flat.

After some plasticy bungling, Sam's voice comes back on the line, now unclotted and resonant: "We'll be there."

I wonder what changed him.

When the contingent from Sam George's house arrives at school just a little late, climbing legs first, like spiders from a cocoon, out of his tiny car, they have lost their conviction. They hide in dark clothing borrowed from Sam, clenched hands burrowing in sleeves so long they could fit only Sam's arms. Eyes fumble; teeth rattle from tiredness.

When Sam Cohen steps out of his own car shortly thereafter, he seems lighter, refreshed, more eager to be there. Gesturing with open arms, he gazes with marvel at the quantity of cars in the lot next to Sam George's. After he spots a friend's car, he ventures indoors to see what's up.

The purpose of name-tagged students—mostly strangers—milling around the lobby of the school loses all importance, though, when he spots a tableful of doughnut boxes, stacked akimbo. He eyes their contents longingly, but he knows he can't eat now, just before practice.

"Take one for later," I suggest.

"Should I?" He glances coyly around the room, but he sees that the other students are wiping sugar from their fingertips and jelly from their lips quite contentedly, their morning hunger satiated.

After Sam counts out six doughnuts, placing them in a box, he tucks the parcel tightly and stealthily into the concavity of his torso and slips from the building.

Seeing Sam's booty, the others perk up, feeling the morning is more purposeful: they have a goal toward which to run. They watch approvingly as Sam locks the stolen sweets in the trunk of his Volvo then double-checks the lock, ensuring the doughnuts are safe.

In my car, we drive to Louise Moore Park, Sam George and Dave bickering about the quality of several recent films. By the time we get there, Sam George and his crew have again reverted back: they walk stiffly and apprehensively toward the running trail. Mostly senior boys, I notice, save Samantha; the freedom that age and cars grant also imposes the burden of running. Doughnuts in mind, though, Sam Cohen remains chipper. To guide our speed workout, he volunteers the application of his futuristic watch. "I got it at Wal-Mart," he reports cheerfully, holding the watch up to his close-set eyes.

While the rest rub thighs and forearms to keep warm, he takes a few minutes to program it, punching at the various buttons as if preparing for an Apollo launch. When he is finished, he lets out a cheer then explains: the alarm will go off at fifteen- and forty-five-second intervals for sprints and recovery.

Despite Sam Cohen's energy, they begin their run just as they did on our first morning in August: waiting for it to end.

Following the wood-chip trail, we start the initial forty-five seconds slow. The morning is rye-colored and damp. Layers of clouds crisscross the sky like skeins of a mop. Running shoes, compressed from a season of use, smack the wood chips hard, pressing those pale bones of trees deep into the damp earth beneath.

When the alarm of Sam Cohen's watch sounds its space-age beep, wood chips fly. All the fear, frustration, and ennui that fuel the desire for practice to end are completely exhaled, and the only thing that replaces them, in both mind and body, is air. As we sprint, the world around us shrinks to contain nothing but the familiar sounds of breathing.

I wonder what changed them.

As we loop round the mile-long path once, twice, and a third time, sprinting, slowing, sprinting, slowing, Dave gets farther and farther away from the rest of us. I don't know whether Dave is finding his stride or the rest are losing theirs. As I watch him, though, he looks no different from the Dave of August; he moves on cat feet, arms tight against his rib cage. The others, too, are exactly the same: Sam George high-fisted and ostrich-eyed, Samantha open-palmed and open-armed.

Only Sam Cohen has changed since August. No longer the burdened boy who stood, without food or hunger, in my living room, he now seems to feel no pain. At the sounds of the alarm, he calls out, *"Go!"* and *"Stop!"*, shouting louder and louder to the increasingly distant Dave until his voice is hoarse.

At the end of the fourth loop, we sprint hard to the place where we began. Gasping, we double over, hands nearly touching the earth. Steam rises from the back of Dave's shirt. Samantha's shins are alive with droplets of sweat.

"That was a good workout," I say, straightening.

Sam Cohen looks at me reproachfully. "It got sort of

hard calling up to Dave," he says. I instantly feel guilty, then realize he is only teasing. When I grin at him he joins in. The others, too, laugh appreciatively. I think: he hasn't changed at all; his smile, as ever, crowds his eyes, his lean frame arcs forward. No, in leaving the pain and associated fear of injury behind, he has just resumed being himself.

No one really changes. Rather, over time, through either training or atrophy, we exaggerate one element of ourselves, let it drape us like Christmas lights so that it seems as if that one quality is our defining characteristic. But other sparks smolder beneath, waiting their turn to be ignited.

As we drive away from the park, our hunger over-whelms us, smothering all other embers. Back at school, we plunder the depths of Sam Cohen's trunk.

"I call the Boston cream," says Dave.

Sam George, who is at a distance, pulling on a sweatshirt, flies around the car, faster than Dave could go, intent only on the doughnut for which he had run earlier. He glares at Dave who grins right back, all-knowing. Sam snatches the coveted doughnut with deft fingers, still eyeing Dave suspiciously. Dave steps aside, his grin escalating to a laugh.

Dave, I realize, struck the match that brought them here. Though he is not Superman, with no comic-book flash or magic, he has the strength to carry his friends along while he runs.

The doughnuts, a few hours stale, have a solidity that grounds us. We eat, filling up on more than air.

Of the elements that comprise our lives—earth, water, fire, air—the last is the least tangible. Only the abstractions of science tell us air is there, coupled with the inexplicable way we sense the presence of all things intangible, like love. All those elements play a role in our lives, but I have a feeling that we are most like air: unable to grasp, to hold, to change.

So Samantha and the boys might run like the unnamed messenger from Marathon, that original, airy runner, in the Penn-Jersey League Championship, or they might be blown away.

NOW, THEY ARE FLOTSAM, adrift in the world.

The day before the Penn-Jersey League Championship, the boys appear with guitars, Samantha her clarinet, and Oliver a script. They are preparing to audition for Coffeehouse, the student talent show, Dave in the corner of the lounge, his electric guitar slung high across his chest, Oliver in the center, trying out his lines on passing girls. Though the school day is over and cross country practice is about to begin, they are slow to leave their art, enter the cold, and form our misshapen warm-up circle.

"Come on, Oliver," I urge.

"I have to memorize my lines," he tells me, his lips drooping sheepishly.

"Are they funny?" I ask. "Do something funny for Coffeehouse."

"Ms. Pont, I'm never funny. You're the only one who finds me funny."

Perhaps he's right; perhaps I don't see things as they are. As I wonder why I find him so amusing, he reaches out for a stray pincurl of my hair and tugs. "Curly . . . straight," he says in his cartoonish voice. He tugs again. "Curly . . . straight." And I bubble with laughter, just as he expected.

When they wistfully put their instruments and words away and step outside, they are pleasantly surprised. It is a warmer day than expected, the air calm and brown. The milky sunshine is muted by pewter clouds. Because all the other teams have completed their seasons, the campus is our own island, a luxury on a rare day like today. As we stretch, everyone turns around themselves like cats, interested only in comfort.

Leyla is sitting, legs stretched in front of her, balanced on hands placed to the left and the right. She is pointing one foot then pulling it back, pointing the other and pulling it back, up and down in a rhythmic, playful, entirely useless motion.

Sam George is telling Samantha a private anecdote that he repeats in her ear to evoke new rushes of giggles from her. As her shoulders shake, she puts up her hands to make him stop, but he keeps talking and talking, she laughing and laughing.

Dave and Bryan, imitating guitar riffs in the air, discuss their Coffeehouse numbers. Their hair bobs up and down to the sound of music in their heads.

Katie and Kristy stare, doe-eyed, at the shimmering sky but don't see a thing.

No one is paying a bit of attention to their stretching. That they have a race tomorrow is beyond comprehension. Tomorrow exists on the other side of an ocean of time.

This afternoon the members of the team seem to be the only ones in the entire world outside of windows. Everyone else, on the inside, is drinking hot chocolate and hot tea, pulling on sweaters, beginning their long hibernation. This last race the team is preparing to run is an afterthought. The earth clinging to their sneakers, just beginning to freeze, is heavy. Pulled down by its weight, they move like creatures whose age has passed.

Finished with their decrepit stretching routine, they are beyond coaching; without my having to say a word, they begin their laps around the campus. They float off, feet skimming the foam-colored tips of the uncut grass, overgrown in these eerily warm days of early November.

Funneling behind the pine tree at the Ballards' house, they are still conversing, unconscious that this is an end. They gossip and giggle over the day's issues, unaware that the painted lines of the course are fading, that the trees are ash-colored and bare.

Gretchen doesn't notice that the soccer and field hockey goals have been dismantled, that no one is there to watch her, even if they knew how. Her large eyes, her swift nose, and her mocha skin belong to August. Since then, she has not changed: she is still beautiful because she wants so badly to run.

Katie and Kristy don't notice that the geese have stripped the pond clean and flown away, taking their hunger to warmer climates. They run alongside each other as they did in early September: for every step Katie takes with her seabird legs, Kristy's muscular calves shuffle through two and a third, yet they remain together.

All around us, fall is tumbling down, stripping the world of color, texture, and sound. I want to say to everyone, "Look, this is the end of everything we have worked for." But I cannot break the silence of November. So they continue to float above the earth, though I want them to stomp it down, to establish dominion over it: to find purpose in running.

Not only do I want them to change—here and now—but I also want to know why three months of training and racing hasn't brought change about.

With no thoughts for tomorrow's race in their minds, I ask myself: Why do they run?

Before I can, in turn, ask them, they race off to practice their guitar riffs, to audition under white spotlights, to wait anxiously for lists of callbacks.

As I walk, again, through school, Leyla rushes up to me. Tears have swollen her eyes; droplets quiver on the rim of her lips.

"Ms. Pont," she says, "someone wrote something mean on my book."

"Oh, Leyla."

I look at her—at who she is—because I have never before considered that an ounce of meanness could enter her life. I know I have only sought, as best I could, to love her. Now, she shakes inside my arms.

I say, "Whoever wrote that is so stupid that you can't take them seriously."

When she doesn't respond, I know she has changed, and I can do nothing about it. That which is elemental about Leyla, that which she would never, could never jettison has been her own love for the world. Some fool, in one streak of scribble, has changed her. I feel her hardening inside my arms, becoming brittle, chilly.

I hug Leyla for as long as she will let me, but no amount of hugging will change her back.

Though I want Leyla and the others to be grounded, there is no firm earth on which to stand; it is as unsupportive as water. The idea of the elements is an abstraction; even earth, water, fire, and air are not what they appear to be.

So I don't know what ground they will run on to-morrow in the Penn-Jersey League Championship and what ground will hold them up as they walk away from glory or disappointment.

OLIVER RISKS THE FURY of the bus driver by staggering on sea legs to the front of the bus in order to sit with me. Crouching in the aisle, he shares a poem he has written entitled "Ode to Cross Country." It begins:

> *Around mid-August, the training had begun*
> *but through lots of work we still had fun*
> *Cross-country, nothing is funnier*
> *Espically with all our runners.*

Before I can comment on spelling or meter, the bus driver chases Oliver to the back of the bus.

There, he is consumed, bodily, by a bonfire of noise that roars and snaps. Eruptions and explosions of joy and mock anger confetti everyone on the bus, back and front, throughout the entire ride to the Solebury School, the site of the Penn-Jersey League Championship. Even inside the bell jar of my Walkman, I cannot escape the heat of their fun. So I take my Walkman off and melt in the strong sunshine refracting through the windows.

I have given up forcing them to be something they're not; nevertheless, I am fearful, right to my core, of what that means for the league championship.

After the bus pulls into the Solebury School parking

lot and we parade in our red wind pants and white shirts to the beginning of the cross country course, we see that other teams, friends, and family have already gathered. In the bowl of the field, everyone can see one another: parents, coaches, runners. At home and on nearly all other courses, except the impenetrable Jim Thorpe, the runners draw along the watchers, who follow at a distance. Here, runners and watchers are face-to-face. Gretchen smiles at her mother, Sam George at his father.

Though the parents keep themselves apart in deference to the seriousness of the event, their faces—pale above dark collars—contain elements of other faces. Looking from Oliver to his mother, from Sam George to his father, now returned from his travels, and from Kristy to her mother and father, I see fractions of the older stitched into the fabric of the younger. The parents gaze on with guarded pride, knowing they are watching some part of themselves. Though they may see what they, in their sons and daughters, have created, at this point, they cannot change a thing.

The four elements are too rarefied by themselves; when they mingle, they create or fuel other things. As they look on their creations, the parents, perceiving the mingling, see mud most of the time, but every once in a while, they catch the leap of flame fed high by air.

So, keeping their distance, Oliver's mother, Sam George's father, and Kristy's mother and father expect to witness a flicker of light, all the while hoping for a show of pyrotechnics.

Nimish and Rajeev are spiraling along the field, chasing each other as a dog chases its own tail. Sam George, presiding over a group of acolytes, is taking sport with Oliver, who turns it on the freshmen. Leyla, rolling along the side of a hill, is, again, her old flower-child self.

Pyrotechnics seem unlikely.

Because the league meet includes a junior varsity race, everyone on the team is dressed to run. Over his uniform, Dave, instead of his Superman shirt, wears the one he designed with the blue toothpaste tube. The younger runners dutifully follow suit. Washed once or twice, the T-shirts have shrunk to size.

Together, we walk Solebury's course, even the veteran boys. The route consists of a twice-repeated loop that begins on a soccer field, feeds into woods, spills onto a road, flanks the front of the school, hugs some school buildings, and crosses a bridge that leads back to the soccer field. It ends where it begins. The only thing, really, that marks the difference between the beginning and the end is the passage of time.

The younger runners like the circularity of the course: they know they won't get lost.

As they walk, they all question the path, wondering how long to stay on the road before stepping onto the grass in the front of the school, how close to certain trees they are allowed to be, and on which side of a vegetable garden they should run.

"Which side is *faster*?" Samantha asks.

"They're both the same," I say.

"Then which side should we take?" Leyla joins in.

"The side you will have to yourself."

As if I am speaking in Zen koans, they look at me, annoyed. They don't want riddles; they want answers.

"Take the side away from whomever you're running against."

"Why?"

"It'll freak 'em out."

The girls all nod in unison. Intimidation makes good strategic sense. Their faces are set, unsmiling. Is this, I wonder, who they are?

Once we arrive at the end—the beginning—they start their stretching. Oliver approaches me. "Prepare the samurai for battle," he says, handing me an elastic band as he has done for the past several races.

Because I have to reach my hands up and he to turn his head down, I have new evidence that Oliver has grown. Though the added bulk makes him seem more mature, more grounded, he has the same teal shadows under his chin and his arms that he had in August, and his pale skin is the same pink in the afternoon sun. After I have doubled the elastic band around a brush of his hair so that it stands up straight, he reaches for a curl of mine to tug.

The younger runners, in their uniforms, jump up and down as they cheer, excited to be watching, excited to be running, excited to be watched. They were not prepared for these feelings.

Gretchen, though, is still tense. Despite the warm tea air, she wraps her wind pants tightly around her shoulders.

Kristy places a hand between her shoulder blades, whispers something in her ear and makes her smile. Whether she casts or breaks a spell is uncertain, but certainly whatever she is saying is magical: her words bring about change.

For Oliver, Gretchen, Kristy, and the rest of them, younger or older, time changes very few things.

The Solebury coach announces the scheduling: boys' varsity in ten minutes; girls' varsity and junior varsity in fifteen minutes. The boys' and girls' races will overlap.

Peeling off layers, the boys expose skin as pale as crustless bread to the colorless sky. As they squint in the sun, the air around them bubbles as if they are underwater. They are floating, not above the world but in it, as if they are waiting to be born. As the varsity boys go through their warm-up run, the girls loll around the moist fields a little longer, never wanting these pleasant sensations to end.

The seven varsity boys find their place on the line among the eight other teams in our league. The white tanks and red shorts of their uniforms, washed too often in some cases, too little in others, fit improperly. Their expensive sneakers, Nike and Reebok, are indistinguishable under the spatterings of mud. After a few sprints, they fall into their joking banter that lasts right up until the official silences them and the gun goes off.

Frightened, I run to the mile mark.

As Dave flies down the paved hill, alone, ten seconds in front of the second-place runner from Girard, dust from the road churns. His downy arms and legs are high, almost arcing. Somewhere, up in the woods where no one could see, Dave completely exhaled all the fear, frustration, and ennui that fuel the desire for a race to end. The only thing left in him, as far as I can tell, is air.

Elated, I run back to the starting line.

On the line, the seven varsity girls look skinny and weak. The junior varsity runners, lined up behind the girls, fidget and whine. Katie's nose is far too small. Kristy, arms crossed, is pouting. Samantha's braids are childish. She fiddles with her hair and the other girls with their uniforms right up until the official silences them and the gun goes off.

Frightened again, I run to the mile mark.

As Samantha hurtles down the paved hill, alone, fifteen seconds in front of the runner from Akiba, pebbles from the road fly up from her feet. Her body is folded inward, pointing forward. Only her hands are, as usual, open, but they churn against her sides like the gears of a train. Somewhere, up in the woods where no one could see, Samantha completely exhaled all the fear, distraction, and childishness that feed the desire for a race to end. The only thing left in the transparent shell of her body is fire.

Elated, I don't move. The whole team is in motion at once, all around me, moving around the circular course, moving away from and moving toward the same point.

At the two-mile mark, Dave is running so quickly that he looks slightly apologetic. He is half a minute in front of the second-place boy. His birdlike tufts of hair are waxy with sweat. His hands loose, his thin fingers appear to be snapping. His joints click along with a primal rhythm, in time with the unchanging rat-a-tat of his feet.

That is who he has always been.

At the two-mile mark, half a minute in front of the second-place girl, Samantha runs open-palmed, still. Otherwise, she reveals a part of herself that we have never seen before. Her perfect smile is gone. She runs like a brushfire, certain of one thing only: that she must keep moving forward. That toothed animal was always in her, fiery as the core of the earth.

One of her braids spontaneously comes undone.

Oliver's hair bobs and weaves like a flame, but remains standing for the duration as if sheltered by an unseen hand cupped around it.

Leyla and Gretchen move as if they are levitating above the world and it is rotating beneath them in the opposite direction.

One after the other, Dave, Bryan, Tom, Oliver, Sam George, Sam Cohen, Samantha, Nimish, Leyla, Gretchen, Holly, Katie, Kristy, and Kate Webbink round the corner by the science classrooms, pass alongside the vegetable garden, cross the bridge, and enter the chorus of cheering at the finish line.

Dave wins the boys' race with a time of 17:12; Samantha wins the girls' race with a time of 20:02; the boys' team places second; the girls' team wins for the first time in the history of Moravian Academy. For the first time in the history of Moravian Academy, five Moravian girls walk to the winners' table at the end of the race for their bit of metal, a squall of applause, a halo of fame. Three boys, too, find themselves striding to the tableful of medals to enter their own rings of light.

"Congratulations, coach," a voice says.

But I can't see. There are tears in my eyes and pictures in my imagination: For the first time in the history of Moravian Academy, I think, runners, male and female, will be noticed by everyone.

I am pulled from my reverie by a dozen or so young arms. Like an autumn day in which every bright leaf falls at once in a shower of pyrotechnics, the joy is madness.

They don't know how they ran so well; they don't know why. The body, sometimes, makes its own choices, regardless of the dictates of the mind. Its needs are just as profound as those of the mind, and its poetry is just as stirring. Nature conjures beauty; our emotions sense it; our imaginations frame it; but the body is the beauty that knows and frames itself.

Its hunger, at times, makes it unstoppable.

In the parking lot of McDonald's, many of the runners, still wearing their medals, snatch doughnuts from a white pastry box Tom Schoeninger holds at arms' length. Then, with powder on their cheeks, they enter McDonald's for the next round.

The long row of tables at which we sit takes on the air of a medieval feast: trays piled high with fries and nuggets of chicken become common property, passed, with a whisper or a joke, from person to person for hands to plunder. The younger runners are sent to fetch refills on beverages. As the tables become more boisterous, I wait for someone to break into song.

But someone is already singing—one of the girls—and her song weaves through the jokes, the insults, and the sounds of chewing, holding all the elements together.

On the way home, I listen to my Walkman for a while, but I crave, for this last time, the sound of voices, the squeals, the assaults, Kristy's gentle reminders, Dave's incongruities, Oliver's absurd flirtations, Nimish and Rajeev's separate language.

Outside the window of the bus, I see a family of deer feeding in an open field. The dark yellow of their hide is the color of the grass, the color of the dead leaves along the side of the road, the color of the last rays of the sun, setting behind an olive hillside. They look up, just for a moment, to blink at our bus, then continue eating, unafraid.

Hope has guided me through so much of this season, warding off its doppelgänger fear, successfully for the most part. Now, I have a hope that is as ungrounded as air, but I will continue running on it, through the winter, spring, and summer, to next fall:

I hope Oliver, Nimish, Gretchen, and Leyla return to me, fragile as origami birds who dream of running on air.

Afterword, Silence

The day after the league race, as I run alone, I reacquaint myself with my own body.

First, I listen to myself breathe. The crunch of broken glass, the groaning of spade-fed leaf blowers, cries of lost geese, and the grinding gears of flatbed trucks all mute as my lungs and heart strike their notes. The snap of valves, the bubbling of intestines, the click of cartilage amplify. My nerve endings emit a steady hiss. For two months, I had forgotten the whir, screech, and hush of my own body in listening to the sounds of those around me. They were a noisy crew.

Yes, I discover, I am all here, breathing the nutmeg-colored air, staining my turtleneck with a champagne of sweat. I love to run, race or no, on roads that are so familiar to me, even alone.

But I also feel tired, changed, heavy. I am glad that no one is here to watch me. Though Oliver, Leyla, the Sams, and Gretchen see me with forgiving eyes, they would wonder at the Tilt-a-Whirl of my first run alone. Runners are so often injured, either in body or mind; they are always trying to recover from that which prevents them from running fast and light.

I am recovering, now, from a season of coaching. In the Zen garden of winter's first chill, I reacquaint myself not just with my own body, but also with the necessity of making it go on its own, no Dave or Samantha to pull me along.

It is hard to find purpose. Though I am only a mile from school, I scuff the hoary shoulder of the flat, open road, struggling to lift my knees. A car on the road swerves into the next lane in an exaggerated move to avoid me, and I wonder if I look as if I will topple over.

We all—Dave, Samantha, Oliver, Leyla, and me—started running because we had to do *something:* to fill a requirement, to fill time, to fill the void created when friends scampered off to play field hockey or soccer. As we continued our running, though, it became everything. The purpose, slowly, defined itself: to win.

Now, the season over, another void opens for me, the type that is left by the absence of myths. I believed in the team, in their ability to win. I need to believe, once again, in myself.

So I have to redefine my purpose; I have to recover from love to learn to be alone. It is an age-old problem, and an ugly one, to boot. It does not wish to be watched.

Last night, at the fall sports awards, I was being watched by parents, athletes, and other coaches. Just off the bus from the Penn-Jersey League Championship, I had slipped into a skirt and blouse squashed from my duffel, but I'd forgotten my makeup. The cross country team looked good, though, still in uniforms, armed with an arsenal of trophies and medals. Sam George, waving spidery arms, staked out a block of wobbly plastic seats in the center of Moravian Academy's auditorium. They all filed in. Flanked by field hockey and soccer players in J. Crew clothing, clean hair, and designer cologne, they looked more exciting: thirty boys and girls exactly matched in red wind pants and white T-shirts with blue toothpaste tubes across the front. As a group, they hung tight not out of shyness but because they knew no one else, at that moment, was up to snuff. They had the hardware cradled like bouquets in their arms to prove it.

I waved at them longingly as I made my way to the

front. They waved back, laughing a bit because I had work to do still, but their long task was done.

After I sat, flattening my skirt with the palm of my hand in a vain attempt to undo the damage of my duffel, men in jackets and ties greeted the audience. I shuffled through the notes of my presentation. Whenever I heard the patter of applause, I looked up and clapped dutifully then returned to my notes.

To close the opening remarks, one administrator stood a little longer. He praised the boys' soccer and the girls' field hockey teams as the heart of Moravian Academy athletics, not only for their seasons—each team had done well in their leagues—but also for their long histories. Lips pursed, I glanced around. Pride gurgled up, airy, from parents and coaches around me. Shiny snapshots in their imaginations offered memories of the games, goals, assists, penalty shots, offense and defense of the season just ended.

I caught the administrator's eye. He stuttered out, "And cross country."

But he didn't mean it. His desire was to praise the more measurable sports—those with plays, ties, overtime, and numbers on the lit-up scoreboard—the sports more easily watched.

It's not his fault that no one understands running. It is a secret sport, one of leaving and returning. I was foolish earlier to think that for the first time in the history of our school male and female runners would be noticed by everyone. Not everyone knows how to make the pilgrimage to a cross country race. The respect, I told myself, might come over time, but those who watch would always, I suspected, be a selective bunch.

Nevertheless, I glanced over my shoulder to see how Sam George and the others had taken that administrator's comment. Their torsos were tight and their faces set, but it was because they were stifling secret laughter. Not wanting to share their secret, they turned their eyes neither left nor right. They had been waiting for this moment since August, had been moving toward it, deliberately and painstakingly. Having at long last arrived, they would allow nothing to penetrate the sacred place at the end of their season.

My turn to take the stage came. There was no microphone, and I was terrified that no one would hear me. I shouted from a plywood podium, and the runners lined up beside me, one by one, as I gave out varsity and junior varsity letters. The team stood along the brink of the stage while I praised and teased them, alternately. The audience laughed with me, and "awwwwed" when Gretchen embraced me.

I gave a few awards, hating their limitations. Dave and Samantha won Most Valuable Runner honors; Nimish and Kate Webbink Most Improved; Holly and Oliver the Coach's Award. Bryan, Katie, and Mike were named captains for next season. I was granted a few minutes to describe the high points of the season, including the remarkable fact that every member of the team—even those who sustained injuries—steadily improved their time for a 3.1-mile course by at least one minute, and over half the team improved their time by over two minutes. Nevertheless, there was not enough time to capture the character of the team the way I wanted to.

There is never enough time to praise people. Time is the foe of all who love. I left the awards ceremony feeling that, though the stopwatch sees things as they truly are, it does not express a thing.

Now, a day after the cross country season's end, I run in an early winter world that is broken-down like an old jalopy. Only a few danger-loving geese linger on the pond; the cornfields are nitrous stubble; the clouds, drooping above my head, are too tired to let loose rain. Often I run to forget, but now I run to remember, to make a pilgrimage backward.

Running along these time-rutted streets of Bethlehem Township, I think about persons and personality: Gretchen's beauty, Oliver's warmth, Dave's enigmatic brilliance, Samantha's shining toughness. All that, and they run, too. Why? The answer, superficially, is to win and to meet goals based on distance and time. I think back to Oliver, after the race against Warren Tech and Belvidere, bolting around to spectators and teammates exclaiming, "Can you believe it? Samantha broke twenty!" and Kristy and Katie, walking away from the line, having no problems believing it.

Samantha's accomplishments and Oliver's declarations of them are the most obvious reasons why people run.

Those are the stories we seek to remember, those of success. But those are not the stories that properly illustrate our lives. Those of pain—Bryan's limp, Leyla's blisters, Sam George's velvet ankle—and those of silliness—the rainy day the team got muddy, purposefully, and Tom was crowned the King of Mud—cut closer to the reality, and even to the pleasure, of doing something as difficult as running.

I am running more comfortably, picking up the pace on springy turf along the side of the road about two miles from school. I have told the team to rest at least two weeks. Some of the seniors will rest longer, maybe forever. In time, they will imagine running only with the vaguest of nostalgia. Some, though, like me, will keep going, trying to find their stride in the silent winter months.

I wish Sam Cohen would. He has all the potential in the world and has yet to realize it. Moreover, if he runs, I know that I will be able to keep him in sight.

On the bus last night, just before arriving home for sports awards, I leaned over the seat in front of me and asked Sam Cohen, "How would you feel if I wrote a book about the cross country team?"

He raised his eyebrows. "Would you change our names?"

"Why would I do that?"

That got him thinking. He turned around and jostled with the others on the bus.

But I understood his question. He was afraid, I suspected, that because he didn't win he wouldn't come off well; because he didn't win, he forgot he is a fine person.

Liquid streetlight poured through the windows of the bus. I could see Sam's cheekbones, like lavender snow, and the relaxed slouch of his shoulders. Though he didn't win, he was happy. He ran well, finished the season better than he thought he would, journeyed through the morass of injury and left, at last, pain behind. He looked forward to going home and telling his friends, Kirsh, Clayton, and Scott, all about it.

To win, really, is to surpass, not others, but ourselves.

I'm a quarter mile from the entrance of Louise Moore Park, moving more swiftly, the air silent—no birds, no cars, no Sams. The balls of my feet just touch the ground so that I am aloft, a part of the silence.

I know, intimately, what Sam was feeling on that bus: peace. The peace that comes when the race is over, when you accomplish that which you set out to do, when you can acknowledge others but thank only yourself. In the auditorium last night, that peace pacified any negative emotion, brought on by administrators or otherwise, as if with a layer of dew. An ounce of meanness meant nothing up against the peace the runners felt in and among themselves.

That peace drifts like mist into the rest of life, giving it a sheen that deflects other meannesses.

As I enter the driveway at Louise Moore Park, watching a squirrel scramble beneath parked cars, I understand that peace but don't wholly feel it. Something is gnawing at me. My season isn't over.

I hear feet on the wood-chip trail behind me. Without looking back, I immediately speed up.

The point is to be better than you thought you could be. That, really, is winning. On a curve of the trail, I sneak a look at the person who was threatening to pass me; he is a hundred yards back. I feel first surprise, then a keen sense of satisfaction.

But not as much, I'll admit, as I felt every time I watched Samantha run well.

I need to keep watching; I am a runner and a watcher simultaneously, and so I feel the conflicting needs to move both forward and back. Even now, on my own, my runners are drawing me along. So, because they have stopped, I have to go back in time and remember: Katie's pale thighs, Kristy's pale calves, Nimish and Rajeev's dark eyes.

Along the wood-chip trail, images of the past months cloak the landscape around me. Memory can't replace actuality, but it will, at least, keep time from robbing me, a little bit, of my desire to keep running.

As I leave Louise Moore Park, I find I am no longer alone. An old man in a green shirt, head like an apple, one of the caretakers, driving a green tractor, smiles and waves. He knows me as the lady who runs. Sometimes he stops his tractor, looks at his watch, and times my loops. Breaking the silence of my solitary runs, he reports exuberantly, at my completion of a loop, minutes and seconds, as if I had broken some record.

He doesn't know that, sometimes, I run for him.

All we want is to be watched, admired, loved. We want the silence of solitude broken by affection. When we earn that love and admiration, we have truly won.

I stop in front of my door, bend over, hands on knees, and breathe deep. My run over, I wonder: What does the Hindu desire after she has plunged into the Ganges? Hope to do it again.

That is why Leyla, Oliver, Dave, and Samantha will keep on running. They know someone is watching, out of love. And that is why I will keep on watching; it is better to love than to be loved.